Contents

KV-635-332

Introduction

I really enjoy entertaining and would happily have people to eat (and drink) with me almost every day of the week. It is just that after a while my bank manager would start objecting, as there is no getting away from the fact that entertaining is an expensive hobby, whether you are giving a dinner party, children's birthday party or a barbecue. However, there are all sorts of ways in which you can cut the costs, without *appearing* to be mean, and this is the real art of successful economical entertaining.

After this book has been published I may well find I haven't any friends left. They will all realise the Scrooge-like way in which I have been treating them, which I am sure (or at least I hope) they didn't notice at the time; filling them up with plenty of good fresh bread, serving a filling soup as a starter, using very cheap cuts of meat disguised in some way, using evaporated milk in a sweet mousse or soufflé where it does not affect the flavour, replacing cream with yogurt in some recipes, using only vegetables which are in season, serving only a good but limited cheese board, etc.

Economical food is often thought of as being dull and stodgy and/or rather complicated; it needn't be either. Pies, flans and dishes containing potatoes and pasta are obvious choices, but they need not be heavy and there is certainly no need for them to be dull, provided you season them well, use fresh or dried herbs for flavouring and add other interesting ingredients. Although some of the dishes require rather more attention than, say, cold lobster, or grilled fillet steak, this does not mean that they all need a great deal of lengthy preparation and cookery expertise. The ability to shop sensibly and to be flexible is far more important than a great deal of cookery knowledge. It is only too easy to go out with a preconceived idea of exactly what you are going to buy so that you can cook a certain dish, only to find that it is either unavailable, or has shot up in price without your realizing it, and this is where you must be prepared to make last minute adjustments and substitutes, if necessary.

Any book on economy suffers from the obvious flaw that, by the time it has been published, some of the food that was economical at the time it was written, may have quite unexpectedly become almost a luxury. Apart from the Common Market and various economic disasters, the weather has a profound effect on prices, mainly of course on fruit and vegetables. Also, after a drought the price of meat may increase because the animals have not put on sufficient flesh through having poor grazing; or after a wet summer the high cost of animal fodder can push up prices. In the winter of 1976, after the long summer drought, potatoes and brussels sprouts, usually the cheapest of vegetables, cost a king's ransom and one would have laughed at any so-called penny-pinching recipe using them.

Economy also largely depends on where you live and your life-style; one of my closest friends recently left suburbia to go and lead the 'good life' in the country and is now surrounded by chickens, ducks, sheep and a pet family cow. For her the most economical dishes are those made with lashings of cream and eggs, and I don't suppose it will be long before fresh asparagus and strawberries are added to her list as well. I have therefore tried to use ingredients which are *generally* cheap for *everyone* whether they live in a town or the country, although there will obviously be some regional, seasonal and yearly fluctuations, and I can't predict too far into the future – after all there was a time when salmon and oysters were only thought fit for the poor!

Suppers and Lunches

It is much easier to get away with cheap food if you have specifically asked friends for 'supper' rather than 'dinner'. For a start, I tend to think of supper as a two-course, rather than a three-course, meal. But even if you are only serving two courses, you want to make sure that people are well fed on food that is satisfying and tastes good, even if it is fairly simple or made from cheap ingredients.

Pastry is a good way of 'extending' meat or fish and there are several recipes for pies in this chapter. At the end of the book, in the Basic Recipes section, I have given my favourite recipe for a quick flaky pastry, which is very easy to prepare but rises well and can be used for a number of recipes in place of home-made or bought puff pastry. Egg and Artichoke Pie, Tavern Pie, and Potato and Pork Pie all make filling but appetizing meals which are just a little out of the ordinary, and you can make all these up in advance, cover the pastry with a piece of self-clinging wrap, and put them into the fridge until you are ready to bake them.

Nice vegetables are equally as important for a simple supper as they are for a dinner party. I have only given a few ideas for vegetables here, but even if you stick to the cheaper root vegetables, cabbages, etc. you can still make very pleasant dishes by adding plenty of seasoning, fresh herbs or some simple sauces. The wide range of dried beans which are now fairly easily available make very good winter vegetables. You can serve any of them in a sauce, such as Butter Beans in Onion Sauce, or they can just be cooked, drained and tossed in a little butter or heated bacon fat with a few pieces of crisp bacon, or in a few tablespoons of French dressing. A hot potato salad is another good, simple vegetable dish – simply boil the potatoes in the usual way, and while they are still warm toss in a few tablespoons of French dressing with a couple of teaspoons of finely chopped onion and some chopped fresh parsley or chives.

For dinner parties I usually serve cold desserts, so that I can make them in advance and forget about them, but for suppers, which are generally much less formal occasions, I rather like hot puddings, and there are some particularly good but simple ones here, such as Pineapple Soufflé Pudding, Wendy's Apricot Soufflé and Belvoir Pudding.

Friends of mine who are not working and whose children are at school all day quite often have two or three people in for lunch, and when I am not too busy I find it is a good way of catching up with everyone's news. Most women don't generally eat a very large lunch and you can simply serve a good home-made soup and follow it with fresh fruit and cheese. However, something light such as the Cheese Pudding (page 25) or Tuna and Egg Salad (page 26) is ideal as these do not require too much preparation in the morning when you are probably trying to do the housework and shopping as well. If the weather is good I can't bear having to eat lunch inside, and some of the recipes from Picnics (page 166) served with salad also make very good, simple lunches for eating out of doors.

Egg and Artichoke Pie

Although I like Jerusalem artichokes I always find them rather a bother to peel, but in this recipe you cook them in their skins and then peel them, which only takes a few minutes.

450 g (1 lb) Jerusalem
  artichokes
salt
25 g (1 oz) butter
25 g (1 oz) flour
1.5 dl (¼ pint) milk
100 g (4 oz) Cheddar cheese,
  grated

2 hard-boiled eggs, shelled
  and chopped
1 tablespoon chopped parsley
freshly milled black pepper
150 g (6 oz) quick rough
  puff pastry (page 188)
milk to glaze

Scrub the artichokes, but do not peel them, and cook in boiling salted water for about 10 minutes until almost tender. Drain, reserving the cooking liquor, and when cool enough to handle, peel and cut into 0.75 cm (¼ inch) thick slices. Melt the butter in a pan, add the flour and cook for a minute, then gradually stir in the milk and 2 dl (generous ¼ pint) of the cooking liquor, and bring to the boil, stirring all the time. Add the cheese and, when it has melted, remove from the heat and stir in the eggs, artichokes and parsley. Season to taste with salt and plenty of pepper. Turn into a pie dish and leave to cool.

Roll out the pastry to an oval slightly larger than the pie dish. Cut a strip about 1.5 cm (½ inch) wide to go round the edge of the dish, damp and place in position. Damp the edges of the pastry and place over the top of the pie filling. Trim the edges, knock-up with the back of a knife and flute. Roll out the pastry trimmings and cut into leaves or flowers for decoration. Brush all over the top with a little milk and bake in a moderately hot oven, 200°C (400°F), Gas Mark 6 for about 30 minutes or until the pastry is golden brown. *Serves 4*

Vol-au-Vent Special

This rather unusual vol-au-vent filling is a very good way of using up left-over chicken or turkey, particularly at Christmas time.

368 g (13 oz) packet frozen
    puff pastry, thawed
6 dl (1 pint) milk
75 g (3 oz) butter or mar-
    garine
1 medium-sized onion, peeled
    and finely chopped
6 rashers streaky bacon, de-
    rinded and chopped

50 g (2 oz) button mush-
    rooms, sliced
50 g (2 oz) flour
150 g (6 oz) cooked chicken
    or turkey, roughly chopped
50 g (2 oz) salted peanuts
50 g (2 oz) seedless raisins
salt
pinch of cayenne pepper

Roll out the pastry to a 22.5 cm (9 inch) square. Trim the edges and knock these up with the back of a knife. Place the square carefully on a damp baking tray. Mark a square all the way round 2.5 cm (1 inch) in from the edge. Cut halfway through the pastry along this line and make a criss-cross pattern over the whole of the top with a sharp knife. Brush with a little of the milk. Bake in a very hot oven 230°C (450°F), Gas Mark 8 for about 10 minutes. Remove the marked square to use as a lid. Place on a separate baking tray and place both trays in the oven for a further 5 minutes or until golden brown and dried out. While the pastry is cooking, melt 25 g (1 oz) of the butter or margarine in a pan and fry the onion, bacon and mushrooms for about 10 minutes. Melt the remaining butter or margarine in a separate pan. Add the flour and cook for a minute. Gradually stir in the milk and bring to the boil, stirring all the time. Add the bacon mixture to the sauce together with the chicken or turkey, peanuts and raisins. Season to taste with salt and cayenne pepper.

    Pour the hot sauce mixture into the hot puff pastry. Place the lid on top and serve as soon as possible. *Serves 6*

Chicken and Ham Pie

I find this useful not only for supper, but for lunch as well, especially if people are bringing their children. The vegetables can be varied according to the season; sometimes I add a drained can of corn, or a packet of frozen mixed vegetables, or young carrots, peas, green peppers or chopped celery or mushrooms if they are cheap at the time. If you have a pressure cooker, both the bacon and the chicken can of course be cooked in this which will save a lot of time.

1 large or 2 small knuckles of bacon, 1 kg (2¼ lb) approximately
1 small bay leaf
1 onion, peeled and chopped
1 sprig thyme
1 teaspoon black peppercorns
1.2 kg (3 lb) boiling chicken (dressed weight)
75 g (3 oz) butter or margarine

75 g (3 oz) flour
9 dl (1½) pints stock (see method)
350 g (12 oz) cooked vegetables (see above)
Salt and freshly milled black pepper
350 g (12 oz) shortcrust pastry (page 187)
beaten egg or milk to glaze

Soak the knuckle for at least 6 hours. If you are a little short of time you can soak it for 4 hours, put it into a pan, cover with cold water, bring to the boil, then discard this water.

Put the knuckle into a pan with the bay leaf, onion, thyme, and peppercorns. Cover with cold water and bring to the boil. Add the chicken, then simmer the pan very gently for about 3 hours or until the chicken and bacon are quite tender. Allow to cool in the cooking liquor if time allows; otherwise, remove the bacon and chicken from the pan, remove the skin of each and cut the flesh into 1.5 to 2.5 cm (½ to 1 inch) dice. Strain the stock and measure off 9 dl (1½ pints).

Melt the butter or margarine in a pan. Add the flour and cook for a minute. Gradually stir in the reserved stock and bring to the boil, stirring all the time. Add the chicken and ham and the cooked vegetables, taste and adjust the seasoning, then turn into a large pie dish and allow to cool.

Roll out the pastry to an oval slightly larger than the top of the pie dish and cut a 1.5 cm (½ inch) strip. Damp the rim of the pie dish and place the strip on top. Damp the strip and place the rolled out pastry over the top. Trim and flute the edges. Roll out the pastry trimmings and cut into leaves to decorate the top. Brush all over the top of the pie with a little beaten egg or milk and bake in a moderately hot oven, 190°C (375°F), Gas Mark 5 for 40 minutes or until the pastry is golden brown. *Serves 8*

Tavern Pie

Steak and kidney pie with a difference, in that the meat is cooked in beer and spiced with some Worcestershire sauce.

2 tablespoons oil
2 large onions, peeled and chopped
450 g (1 lb) stewing beef
225 g (8 oz) ox kidney
40 g (1½ oz) flour
salt and black pepper
3 dl (½ pint) brown ale
1.5 dl (¼ pint) water

¼ teaspoon dried thyme
thinly peeled rind of ½ an orange
1 tablespoon Worcestershire sauce
225 g (8 oz) puff pastry (page 188) or 368 g (13 oz) packet frozen puff pastry
beaten egg or milk to glaze

Heat the oil in a pan and fry the onions for 5 minutes. Cut the beef into 2.5 cm (1 inch) cubes and the kidney into 1.5 cm (½ inch) cubes, discarding any core, and toss in the flour, seasoned with salt and pepper. Add to the pan and cook for about 5 minutes, stirring frequently until the meat is browned. Remove from the heat and gradually stir in the ale and water. Return to the heat and bring to the boil, stirring all the time. Add the thyme and orange rind. Cover the pan and simmer gently for 1½ to 2 hours or until the meat is tender. Remove the orange rind, stir in the Worcestershire sauce, turn into a pie dish and allow to cool.

Roll out the pastry to an oval slightly larger than the pie dish. Cut off a 1.5 cm (½ inch) piece to go round the edge of the pie dish, damp with water and place in position. Cover the pie with pastry, seal the edges, trim and flute. Roll out any pastry trimmings and cut into leaves to decorate the top. Brush all over the top of the pie with beaten egg or milk. Bake in a hot oven, 220°C (425°F), Gas Mark 7, for about 25 minutes or until the pastry is golden brown. *Serves 6*

Potato and Pork Pie

The French are particularly ingenious in the way in which they use vegetables to make delicious but inexpensive meals, and this is an adaptation of an old French dish often called Truffat because potatoes were said to be the truffles of the poor. Although you could use ordinary shortcrust pastry for it, I think it is much nicer made with the French Pâté Brisé below.

For the pastry:
225 g (8 oz) plain flour
pinch of salt
100 g (4 oz) butter or margarine

1 egg
about 2 tablespoons cold water

Sift the flour and salt on to a working surface. Cut the butter or margarine into small cubes. Make a well in the centre of the flour and put in the fat, egg and water. Using your fingertips, work the fat, egg and water into the flour until it is well blended. The dough should cling together, leaving the working surface clean, so you may have to add a little more water (but do not make it too wet). Knead the dough lightly for about 3 minutes, until it forms a smooth ball, then put it into a polythene bag and into the fridge for at least 30 minutes before using.

For the filling:

350 g (12 oz) streaky pork rashers	salt and freshly milled black pepper
1 large onion, peeled and chopped	2 tablespoons chopped parsley
650 g (1½ lb) potatoes, peeled and thinly sliced	1.5 dl (¼ pint) double or single cream

Roll out two thirds of the pastry and use to line a deep 22.5 cm (9 inch) flan ring or tin or shallow cake tin.

Cut the pork into 1.5 cm (½ inch) pieces and put into a mixing bowl with the onion, potatoes, seasoning and parsley and mix well. Put the potato mixture into the pastry case and damp the edges of the pastry with water. Roll out the remainder of the pastry into a circle and place on top of the pie. Seal the edges, then trim and roll out any pastry trimmings and cut into leaves to decorate the top. Make a hole in the centre of the pie about 1.5 cm (½ inch) in diameter for the steam to escape. Bake in a moderate oven, 180°C (350°F), Gas Mark 4 for 1½ hours. Fifteen minutes before the end of cooking, remove the pie from the oven and carefully pour the cream in through the hole in the centre. Replace in the oven and if the pie is becoming a little too brown, cover with foil. Serve hot. *Serves 6*

Buttered Spinach Stalks

If you have never discovered the delights of spinach stalks you are in for a treat. All too often when people prepare spinach they simply throw the stalks away and do not realize that these constitute a delicious vegetable dish in themselves, which can also be served as a starter. The taste is difficult to describe, but there is a hint of asparagus about it and, like asparagus, they can be cooked and served cold in a good French dressing if you prefer. The amount of stalks 900 g (2 lb) spinach yields varies slightly with the kind of spinach and the time of year, but on average you will get about 225 g (8 oz) or just over, which is enough for 3 to 4 people.

225 g (8 oz) spinach stalks   *50 g (2 oz) melted butter*
salt   *freshly milled black pepper*

Trim the stalks as neatly as possible, then tie into two neat
bundles with string. Heat about 2.5 cm (1 inch) salted water
in the base of a large pan. When it is boiling, add the spinach
stalks and cook gently for about 8 minutes or until they are all
quite tender. Drain very well, turn into a serving dish and
pour over the melted butter. Grind plenty of black pepper
over the top and serve as soon as possible. *Serves 3 to 4*

Cheese and Spinach Soufflé

Soufflés make marvellous light lunch or supper dishes and are
nothing like as difficult or complicated as is generally
imagined.

25 g (1 oz) butter or mar-   *4 eggs, separated*
garine   *salt and freshly milled black*
25 g (1 oz) flour   *pepper*
2 dl (scant ½ pint) milk   *a good pinch of grated nut-*
100 g (4 oz) strong Cheddar   *meg*
cheese, grated   *1 teaspoon made mustard*
100 g (4 oz) well drained,
chopped cooked spinach

Melt the butter or margarine in a pan, add the flour and cook
for a minute. Gradually add the milk and bring to the boil,
stirring all the time. Lower the heat, stir in the cheese and
cook gently, stirring, until the cheese has melted. Remove
from the heat and beat in the spinach, then the egg yolks, one
at a time. Add the seasoning, nutmeg and mustard and beat
well. Whisk the egg whites until they form stiff peaks, then
fold carefully into the mixture. Turn into a well-greased 1.5
litre (2½ pint) soufflé dish and bake in a moderately hot
oven, 190°C (375°F), Gas Mark 5 for about 30 minutes or
until well risen and golden brown. *Serves 3 as a main course*

Cabbage, Potato and Pepper Bake

The invention of this recipe was pure chance – I had some Skordalia left over from testing, together with some crudités and also a quantity of leftover cooked cabbage. In desperation for something for the family's lunch I just put the whole lot together into a frying pan, with some bits of bacon, and fried it all up and the result was so good I felt it was worth developing a proper recipe for it.

900 g (2 lb) potatoes
salt
juice of 1 lemon
3 cloves of garlic, crushed
4 tablespoons oil
freshly milled black pepper
900 g (2 lb) cabbage

225 g (8 oz) streaky bacon,
 de-rinded and chopped
1 large red pepper, seeded
 and sliced
1 large green pepper,
 seeded and sliced

Peel the potatoes and cook in boiling salted water until tender. Drain well and mash with the lemon juice, garlic and half the oil. Beat well and season to taste with salt and pepper. Shred the cabbage finely, discarding the coarse central stalks, and wash in cold water. Cook in boiling salted water until just tender, then drain well. Heat the remaining oil in a large frying pan and fry the bacon until it is beginning to crisp. Remove from the pan with a draining spoon. Add the peppers to the pan and fry gently for 5 minutes, then add to the cabbage and toss lightly together.

Spread half the potato in the base of a large ovenproof dish, top with half the bacon and half the pepper and cabbage mixture. Repeat these layers. Cover the dish and bake in a moderately hot oven, 190°C (375°F), Gas Mark 5 for 45 minutes. Remove the lid 15 minutes before the end of cooking. *Serves 4 to 6*

Cassoulet

This marvellous French peasant dish from the Languedoc is delicious and very filling – ideal for winter suppers.

450 g (1 lb) haricot beans
1.35 litres (2¼ pints) stock
225 g (8 oz) salt pork
225 g (8 oz) stewing lamb
25 g (1 oz) lard or dripping
1 large onion, peeled and
   chopped
2 cloves of garlic, crushed
100 g (4 oz) lean bacon

4 tablespoons concentrated
   tomato purée
1 bay leaf
1 teaspoon mixed dried herbs
225 g (8oz) garlic sausage,
   sliced
50 g (2oz) fresh white breadcrumbs

Soak the beans overnight in cold water. Drain and put into a pan with the stock. Cover the pan, bring to the boil and simmer gently for 1½ hours or until the beans are tender.

Soak the pork for 2 to 3 hours in cold water. Drain and cut into 2.5 cm (1 inch) cubes with the lamb. Melt the lard or dripping in a flameproof casserole and fry the onion, garlic, pork, lamb and bacon for about 10 minutes. Add the beans, together with their cooking liquor, the tomato purée, bay leaf, herbs and garlic sausage. Mix well, cover the pan and cook in a very moderate oven, 170°C (325°F), Gas Mark 3 for about 2½ hours. Sprinkle the breadcrumbs over the top and bake uncovered for a further 30 minutes. *Serves 6 to 8*

Spinach and Pancake Layer

This can be served as a main course for supper, and it also makes a very good starter for a dinner party. If fresh spinach is not in season you can use frozen spinach, or it is also excellent made with sorrel.

3 dl (½ pint) basic pancake
    batter (page 190)
oil or lard for frying
900 g (2 lb) fresh spinach or
    450 g (1 lb) frozen spinach
25 g (1 oz) margarine

salt and freshly milled black
    pepper
225 g (8 oz) curd cheese
3 dl (½ pint) cheese sauce
    (page 189)
50 g (2 oz) Cheddar cheese,
    grated.

Make up the batter and use to make 8 to 10 pancakes, separating each pancake when cooked with a piece of foil or greaseproof paper.

Wash the spinach well in plenty of cold water to remove all the dirt and grit. Melt the margarine in a pan. Add the spinach, season with salt, cover the pan and cook until the spinach is tender. Drain the spinach well and season with salt and pepper.

Place one pancake in the bottom of an ovenproof dish, spread with curd cheese and some of the spinach. Continue these layers, using all the cheese and spinach and ending with a pancake on the top. Pour over the cheese sauce and sprinkle with the Cheddar cheese. Bake in a moderately hot oven 200°C (400°F), Gas Mark 6 for 30 minutes or until the top is golden brown. Serve with wholemeal bread. *Serves 4 as a main course or 6 to 8 as a starter*

Braised Lamb Knuckles

The Greeks have used lamb knuckles or shanks for centuries to make a dish called Kleftiko, which they cooked very slowly over Saturday night, so that the Greek mother did not have to do any cooking on Sunday. Lamb knuckles can now be bought in many supermarkets, and the flavour of this dish is excellent if it is cooked slowly. However, it is not something I would serve to people who are very 'proper' as you really have to pick the bone up in your fingers to eat it to get out all the flavour.

4 lambs' knuckles
538 g (1 lb 3 oz) can
  tomatoes
1 rounded teaspoon dried
  oregano
3 onions, peeled and chopped
2 cloves of garlic, crushed

2 sticks celery, chopped
juice of 1 lemon
salt and freshly milled black
  pepper
50 g (2 oz) black olives
  (optional)

Put the knuckles into a roasting tin or casserole. Turn the tomatoes into a basin and chop roughly. Add all the remaining ingredients and mix lightly together, then pour over the lamb. Cover and cook in a slow oven, 150°C (300°F), Gas Mark 2 for 3 to 4 hours. If you are around it is a good idea to stir the lamb after about 15 minutes' cooking, but this is not essential if you wish to leave it cooking in the oven while you go out, or put it in the oven in the morning and leave the oven to switch itself on automatically. Taste and adjust the seasoning before serving with a rice pilaf. *Serves 4*

Pigeon and Cabbage Casserole

Wood pigeons used to be very cheap, but like most other things have become quite expensive these days. As I like the gamey flavour, I find it is a good idea to eke them out by cutting them in half and cooking them with another meat, such as frankfurters or pork belly. This casserole is very easy as it can just cook away quietly in the oven for hours and I generally serve it with baked potatoes in their jackets to reduce the cooking implements to the minimum.

3 wood pigeons
1 tablespoon oil
450 g (1 lb) cooking apples,
  peeled and diced
450 g (1 lb) onions, peeled
  and chopped
1.3 kg (3 lb) red cabbage,
  shredded
salt and freshly milled black
  pepper

¼ teaspoon grated nutmeg
½ teaspoon ground cloves
4 tablespoons soft brown
  sugar
1.5 dl (¼ pint) wine or cider
  vinegar
1.5 dl (¼ pint) stock
6 large frankfurters or
  knackwurst

Cut the pigeons in half. Heat the oil in a pan and fry them quickly on each side until browned. Put a quarter of the apples and onion into a large casserole, cover with a quarter of the cabbage. Season well and sprinkle with a little of the nutmeg, cloves and sugar. Repeat these layers once, then place the pigeon halves together with the fat from the pan on top, then continue the layers finishing with a layer of cabbage. Mix the vinegar with the stock and pour this over the casserole. Cover and cook in a very slow oven, 150°C (300°F), Gas Mark 2 for 2½ hours. Remove from the oven, bury the frankfurters or knackwurst in the casserole, and cook for a further 30 minutes. Taste and adjust seasoning before serving. *Serves 6*

Spaghetti with Garlic and Bacon

This really is one of the cheapest, most filling, yet most delicious recipes I know. I tend to serve it for supper on Sunday nights and similar occasions, when I feel people have probably had a good protein intake at lunch time, but it can also be served as a starter in slightly smaller quantities. You can use fairly fat bacon or bacon trimmings, in which case you will probably not need the oil and you can vary it by adding anything which you happen to have: an onion, chopped and fried with the bacon, a few chopped mushrooms, some cooked or canned sweetcorn, some chopped cooked sausages or frankfurters etc. To make it into Spaghetti Carbonara, decrease the garlic or omit it altogether, lightly beat 4 eggs and add to the spaghetti when it is hot. Cook lightly, stirring all the time, until the eggs start to scramble round the spaghetti.

450 g (1 lb) spaghetti
salt
350 g (12 oz) streaky bacon
2 tablespoons oil, preferably
*   olive*
4 cloves garlic, crushed

3 tablespoons chopped pars-
*   ley*
To serve:
grated Parmesan, Cheddar or
*   Edam cheese*

Cook the spaghetti in a large pan of boiling salted water until it is just tender; do not overcook it. Drain well. While the spaghetti is cooking, cut off the rind and chop the bacon. If liked, the rind can then be fried in a separate small pan until it is very crisp and crumbled over the top of the spaghetti just before serving. Put the bacon with the oil into a second large pan over a very gentle heat until the fat runs, then fry until crisp. Add the garlic and parsley and plenty of black pepper, then the spaghetti and mix all together very well. Heat for 2 to 3 minutes, then serve as soon as possible with cheese, fresh brown bread and a tossed green salad. *Serves 6*

Home-made Ravioli

People are always highly impressed if you make something yourself which is very often bought completely or at least partially prepared, such as ravioli.

For the pasta:

225 g (8 oz) plain flour
1 teaspoon salt
1 egg
1 tablespoon oil
3 to 4 tablespoons hot water
beaten egg for sealing
For the filling:
1 tablespoon oil
1 small onion, peeled and
grated
225 g (8 oz) lean minced
pork
50 g (2 oz) cooked ham,
minced
salt and freshly milled black
pepper
¼ teaspoon grated nutmeg

a pinch of dried sage
1 egg, beaten
For the sauce:
2 tablespoons oil
100 g (4 oz) bacon pieces,
finely chopped
1 clove garlic, crushed
2 medium-sized onions,
peeled and chopped
2 sticks celery, finely chopped
450 g (1 lb 13 oz) can
tomatoes
1 teaspoon freshly chopped
basil
salt and freshly milled black
pepper

Sift the flour and salt into a bowl and make a well in the
centre. Break in the egg, then add the oil and water. Work to
a dough with your fingertips, adding a little extra water if
necessary. Turn out on to a floured surface and knead for
about 10 to 15 minutes or until the dough is very smooth and
no longer sticks to your fingers. Wrap in a damp cloth and
leave for 30 minutes.

Heat the oil in a pan and gently fry the onion for 5 minutes.
Add the pork and cook, stirring, for a further 5 minutes, then
add the ham, seasoning, nutmeg and sage and cook for a
further 5 minutes. Remove from the heat, beat in the egg and
allow to cool. Mince when cold so that the meat becomes very
fine.

Divide the dough in half and roll out to two rectangles,
approximately 40 x 30 cm (16 x 12 inches), but make one
very slightly larger than the other. Brush all over the small
sheet with beaten egg and put half-teaspoonfuls of the filling
about 2 cm (¾ inch) apart. Cover with the second sheet of

dough and press firmly round each piece of filling to seal the two layers together. Using a pastry wheel or a sharp knife, cut between the little balls of filling to make neat squares. Place in one layer, on a floured tray, flour again and cover with a dry cloth until required.

Heat the oil for the sauce in a small pan and gently fry the bacon for 5 minutes. Add the garlic, onions and celery, and cook gently for another 5 minutes. Add the tomatoes, herbs and seasoning and simmer uncovered for 20 minutes. Cook the ravioli in a large pot of boiling salted water for 5 minutes or until they float to the surface. Drain well, turn into a heated dish and serve with the tomato sauce and grated cheese. *Serves 4 to 6*

Cheese Pudding

I always think that the title of this recipe makes it sound rather heavy and unappetizing, which is far from the truth. The texture is very light, although not quite as light as a soufflé, and it makes an excellent main course for lunch or supper, served with a tomato and tossed green salad, or it could be served as a starter for a dinner party.

100 g (4 oz) fresh white breadcrumbs
4.5 dl (¾ pint) milk
25 g (1 oz) margarine
150 g (6 oz) Cheddar cheese, grated

3 eggs, beaten
salt and freshly milled black pepper
1 tablespoon chopped chives or spring onions

Put the breadcrumbs into a basin. Heat the milk with the margarine, pour over the crumbs and leave for 10 minutes. Add the grated cheese, eggs, seasoning and chives or spring onions and mix well. Turn into a 1.2 litre (2 pint) ovenproof dish and bake in a moderately hot oven, 200°C (400°F), Gas Mark 6 for 30 to 35 minutes or until well risen and golden brown. Serve as soon as possible. *Serves 4*

Tuna and Egg Salad

This is a variation of Salade Niçoise, but made with cooked potatoes and plenty of vegetables to give extra bulk without appearing to be mean!

450 g (1 lb) new potatoes
225 g (8 oz) beans, either French or runner, cut into 5 cm (2 inch) lengths
salt
227 g (8 oz) can sweetcorn, drained
1 small bunch of spring onions, finely chopped

2 sticks celery, finely chopped (optional)
4 tablespoons French dressing
184 g (6½ oz) can tuna
4 hard-boiled eggs, shelled and quartered
4 tomatoes, quartered
1 large lettuce
1 box mustard and cress

Cook the potatoes and beans separately in boiling salted water until just tender. Drain well and cut the potatoes into 0.75 cm (¼ inch) slices. Put into a bowl with the drained sweetcorn, spring onions and celery (if using). Pour over the French dressing, add the oil from the can of tuna and toss lightly together. Leave until the potatoes and beans are quite cold. Flake the tuna and add to the potatoes together with half the eggs and half the tomatoes. Wash and dry the lettuce thoroughly and use to line a large salad bowl. Pile the tuna and potato mixture into the centre and garnish with the remaining tomatoes and egg and the cress strewn over the top. *Serves 6*

Fish Cardinal

I find this makes a very pleasant, light summer lunch or supper and you can use any white fish you like, haddock, cod, whiting, coley, huss, sea bream, brill, etc. If you have any fennel growing in your garden it makes a particularly attractive garnish for this dish.

500 g (1¼ lb) filleted white
   fish
3 dl (½ pint) water
2 slices lemon
1 small bay leaf
few white peppercorns
salt
1.5 dl (¼ pint) soured cream
1.5 dl (¼ pint) thick mayon-
   naise

1 tablespoon tomato purée
1 tablespoon tomato ketchup
few drops of Tabasco
1 teaspoon soy sauce
1 tablespoon lemon juice

To garnish:
lettuce leaves
few sprigs of fennel (optional)
lemon wedges

Place the fish in a pan with the water, lemon slices, bay leaf, peppercorns and a good pinch of salt. Cover and poach gently for about 5 minutes or until the fish is just tender. Allow to cool, then drain and flake, discarding the skin and any small bones. Blend the soured cream into the mayonnaise with the tomato purée, tomato ketchup, Tabasco, soy sauce and lemon juice. Gently fold in the fish. Place the mixture on a serving dish and garnish with lettuce leaves, fennel, if available, and lemon wedges. *Serves 4*

Mussels Cooked in Cider

Mussels are generally served as a starter, but they make an excellent main dish, and you will find that by the time everyone has dunked plenty of French bread into the sauce so as not to waste any, they will be feeling very replete.

4.8 litres (8 pints) mussels
1 onion, peeled and chopped
1 or 2 cloves of garlic
  (optional)
few parsley stalks
1 sprig thyme
1 bay leaf
a few black peppercorns

4.5 dl (¾ pint) dry cider
40 g (1½ oz) butter
40 g (1½ oz) flour
salt
freshly milled black pepper
2 tablespoons chopped parsley

Put the mussels into a bucket of cold water to soak: this removes some of the excess salt and helps reduce the chore of cleaning them. Scrub the mussels with a brush to remove all traces of seaweed, mud and beard. Discard any which are cracked, or are open and do not close when sharply tapped. Put the onion, garlic, if using, parsley stalks, thyme, bay leaf, peppercorns, and cider into a large pan and bring to the boil. Add the mussels, cover the pan and cook gently for about 5 minutes, or until the mussels are open. Remove the pan from the heat, discard the empty half of each shell and put the mussels into a heated serving dish and keep warm. Boil the cooking liquor rapidly until it is reduced to about 9 dl (1½ pints).

Melt the butter in a separate pan, add the flour and cook for a minute. Gradually strain in the cooking liquor and bring to the boil, stirring all the time. Taste the sauce and adjust the seasoning, then pour over the mussels and sprinkle with the chopped parsley before serving. *Serves 6*

Leek, Orange and Watercress Salad

Ideal for any light lunch, this pleasant salad looks attractive and is rather unusual.

650 g (1½ lb) leeks
1 large orange
1 bunch of watercress

1 tablespoon sunflower seeds
2 tablespoons French dressing

Clean the leeks and cut them into 1.5 cm (½ inch) lengths. Steam or boil until just tender, drain and dry well and place in a salad bowl. Peel the orange, discarding all the white pith. Cut out the segments, discarding all the pith, and add to the leeks; do this over the salad bowl, so that any juice goes into the bowl. Trim the watercress, wash and dry well and add to the leeks. Put the sunflower seeds on a piece of foil on the rack of the grill pan and toast until they are golden brown. Pour the dressing over the salad just before serving, toss lightly together and sprinkle with the sunflower seeds. *Serves 4*

Butter Beans in Onion Sauce

It took me years to like butter beans again, having been fed them in their most revolting form at school, and it still surprises me just how nice they *can* taste. If you have a pressure cooker you can of course speed up the cooking process considerably as they will then only need 30 minutes.

225 g (8 oz) butter beans
3 medium-sized onions, peeled and chopped
1 bay leaf
salt and freshly milled black pepper

50 g (2 oz) margarine
25 g (1 oz) flour
2 dl (scant ½ pint) milk
1 tablespoon chopped parsley
a good pinch of cayenne pepper

Soak the beans overnight in cold water. Drain and put into a pan with one of the onions, the bay leaf and seasoning. Cover with fresh cold water, bring to the boil and simmer gently for 2½ to 3 hours or until the beans are quite tender. Drain and reserve the cooking liquor.

Melt the margarine in a clean pan and gently fry the remaining onions for 5 minutes. Stir in the flour and cook for a minute, then gradually stir in the milk. Bring to the boil, stirring all the time, then stir in the beans and the parsley. Season to taste with salt and cayenne pepper and heat gently. If the mixture is a little too thick, stir in a couple of table-spoons of the cooking liquor. Turn into a serving dish when the beans are piping hot. *Serves 6*

Tomato, Onion and Marrow Bake

Marrows are one of the cheapest of all summer vegetables, but unless they are well cooked they can be very unpleasant and watery. To remove some of the excess water peel the marrow, cut into pieces and put in a large colander. Sprinkle with about a teaspoon of salt and leave for an hour, during which time much of the water will come out of the vegetable. Dry thoroughly with kitchen paper and then cook.

1 medium-sized marrow
1 teaspoon salt
1 tablespoon oil
2 medium-sized onions,
  peeled and chopped

450 g (1 lb) tomatoes, peeled
  and chopped
1 sprig of thyme
freshly milled black pepper

Peel the marrow, cut it into 5 cm (2 inch) slices and salt as above. Heat the oil in a fireproof casserole and gently fry the onions for 5 minutes. Add the tomatoes, marrow, thyme and pepper. Cover the casserole and cook in a moderate oven, 180°C (350°F), Gas Mark 4 for 1¼ hours. Taste and adjust the seasoning before serving. *Serves 4 to 6*

Wendy's Apricot Soufflé

This must rate as one of the simplest of all puds to make, and is particularly economical if you have several egg whites left over from making mayonnaise.

350 g (12 oz) jar apricot jam   5 egg whites

Put the jam into a saucepan and heat gently until soft, then remove from the heat. Whisk the egg whites until they form soft peaks, and fold them carefully into the jam. Turn into a lightly buttered soufflé dish and bake in a moderately hot oven, 200°C (400°F), Gas Mark 6 for 25 minutes or until well risen and pale golden. Serve immediately with cream.
  Serves 4 to 6

Pineapple Soufflé Pudding

This pudding separates out on cooking so that you end up with a light, soufflé mixture on the top and a sauce in the bottom of the dish.

50 g (2 oz) margarine
50 g (2 oz) caster sugar
grated rind and juice of ½
  lemon

2 eggs, separated
50 g (2 oz) self-raising flour
2.5 dl (scant ½ pint) pine-
  apple juice

Cream the margarine and sugar with the lemon rind until light and fluffy. Gradually beat in the egg yolks, the sifted flour and the lemon and pineapple juice. Whisk the egg whites stiffly, and fold into the mixture; it will appear curdled at this stage, but this does not matter. Pour the mixture into a 9 dl (1½ pint) soufflé dish and stand in a roasting tin containing 2.5 cm (1 inch) of cold water. Bake in a moderate oven, 180°C (350°F) Gas Mark 4 for 30 to 40 minutes. Serve hot as soon as possible. *Serves 4*

Belvoir Pudding

This is another very light steamed pudding and was the first dish I ever prepared for photography, when I started work for a PR company.

100 g (4 oz) butter or margarine
100 g (4 oz) caster sugar
grated rind and juice of 2
   lemons
2 egg yolks
100 g (4 oz) fresh white
   breadcrumbs

½ teaspoon baking power
For the meringue:
2 egg whites
50 g (2 oz) caster sugar
1 large dessert apple

Cream the butter or margarine, sugar and lemon rind until light and fluffy, then beat in the egg yolks. Fold in half the breadcrumbs, then the lemon juice, the rest of the crumbs and finally the baking powder. Turn into a greased 9 dl (1½ pint) pudding basin, cover with greased foil and steam, either in a steamer or in a saucepan of gently boiling water, for 45 minutes.

Shortly before the pudding is ready, whisk the egg whites until they form stiff peaks and gradually whisk in the sugar, a teaspoon at a time. Peel and core the apple and chop finely. Fold into the meringue, then spread this thickly round the edge of a fireproof serving dish. Put into a moderately hot oven, 200°C (400°F), Gas Mark 6 for about 5 minutes, until just lightly browned, then remove from the oven, uncover the pudding and invert into the centre of the dish. Serve hot. *Serves 4 to 6*

Apple Pan Dowdy

Not the most elegant of puddings, but one that always seems to be popular, especially with men, most of whom seem to secretly love nursery-type puddings!

3 large cooking apples
2 tablespoons soft brown
  sugar
1 tablespoon golden syrup
¼ teaspoon grated nutmeg
¼ teaspoon ground cinna-
  mon

100 g (4 oz) self-raising flour
pinch of salt
50 g (2 oz) caster sugar
1 egg, beaten
50 g (2 oz) margarine, melted
4 tablespoons milk

Peel, core and thinly slice the apples. Put into a 17.5 cm (7 inch) cake tin with the brown sugar, syrup, nutmeg and cinnamon. Cover with foil and bake in a moderately hot oven, 190°C (375°F), Gas Mark 5 for 20 minutes.

Sift the flour and salt into a bowl. Add the sugar, egg, margarine and milk and beat well. Spoon this mixture over the top of the apples and spread evenly. Return to the oven and bake uncovered for a further 30 to 40 minutes or until the cake mixture is pale golden. Invert the tin on to a serving dish and serve hot. *Serves 4 to 6*

Crunchy Apple Crumble

This is a rather pleasant variation on an old favourite.

9 dl (1½ pints) sweetened
  apple purée
150 g (6 oz) wholemeal flour
75 g (3 oz) margarine

50 g (2 oz) roasted buck-
  wheat
50 g (2 oz) demerara sugar

Pour the apple purée into the base of an ovenproof dish. Turn the wholemeal flour into a bowl and rub in the margarine until the mixture resembles fine breadcrumbs. Add the buckwheat and demerara sugar and mix well. Sprinkle over the top of the apple purée. Bake in a moderately hot oven, 200°C (400°F), Gas Mark 6 for 30 minutes or until the top is golden brown. *Serves 4 to 6*

Rhubarb Kisel

Kisel is a Russian dessert, generally made from red berries, such as raspberries, redcurrants, etc., but this is a very pleasant (and much cheaper) variation using rhubarb. Ideally you should use the pink early rhubarb as this gives the dessert a very pretty colour, but you can of course use ordinary garden rhubarb, and add a few drops of red colouring if you wish.

450 g (1 lb) rhubarb	1 level tablespoon cornflour
juice of 1 large orange	a little extra caster sugar
100 g (4 oz) sugar, approx.	

Cut the rhubarb into 5 cm (2 inch) pieces. Make the orange juice up to 3 dl (½ pint) with water and pour over the rhubarb. Add the sugar, cover the pan and simmer the rhubarb gently for about 10 minutes or until it is quite tender. Sieve or purée in a blender. Blend the cornflour with 2 tablespoons of cold water in a basin and bring the fruit purée to the boil. Pour over the slaked cornflour, stirring, then return it all to the pan and bring to the boil, stirring all the time. Taste and add a little more sugar, if necessary. Remove from the heat and pour into a serving dish, sprinkle over a little caster sugar to prevent a skin from forming, then leave until cool. Chill before serving. *Serves 6*

Floating Islands

This is a classic French recipe which is suprisingly cheap, especially when eggs are plentiful. Although you can keep the custard plain, it is nicer if you add a couple of tablespoons of brandy, rum or sherry.

6 dl (1 pint) milk	of vanilla essence
2 large eggs, separated	3 tablespoons water
100 g (4 oz) caster sugar	3 tablespoons granulated
1 vanilla pod or a few drops	sugar

Pour the milk into a shallow pan or deep frying pan and heat to simmering point. Whisk the egg whites very stiffly, and then gradually whisk in half the caster sugar. Drop spoonfuls of the meringue mixture on top of the hot milk. Poach for 2 minutes, then turn with a perforated spoon or spatula and poach for the same time on the second side. Lift the meringues from the milk and drain on kitchen paper.

Beat the egg yolks in a basin with the remaining caster sugar and pour over the milk. Add the vanilla pod or essence and turn into the top of a double saucepan or a basin over a pan of hot water. Cook over a gentle heat, stirring, until the custard coats the back of a wooden spoon. Remove the vanilla pod. Pour into a shallow dish and allow to cool. Top with the meringue balls and chill for about 2 hours. Put the water and sugar into a saucepan over a low heat until the sugar dissolves. Boil rapidly until the mixture turns golden brown, then spoon the caramel quickly over the meringues.   *Serves 4*

Plum Syllabub

This is essentially a seasonal recipe, although it could be made with frozen plums. It can also be made with damsons, but as these are much sharper you must increase the amount of sugar.

450 g (1 lb) plums   *1.5 dl (¼ pint) double cream*
75 g (3 oz) soft brown sugar
  (approximately)

Cut the plums in half and remove the stones. If they are very difficult to remove, they can be left and removed after cooking. Put the plums into a heavy-based pan with the sugar, cover and cook over a very gentle heat for about 15 minutes or until the plums are quite tender. Sieve the plums or purée in a blender and allow to cool. Taste and add a little extra sugar if necessary. Lightly whip the cream and fold into the plum purée, but reserve about 2 tablespoons of the purée for decorating. Turn the syllabub into a dish or individual glasses and chill for at least 1 hour. Just before serving pour over the reserved purée so that it makes an attractive pattern on the top. *Serves 4 to 6*

Autumn Pudding

When I was little we quite often used to go and stay with my aunt and uncle who lived in a beautiful old mill on the Essex/Suffolk border, and I have a very vivid memory of eating this for breakfast one morning! I imagine it must have been left over from the adults' supper the night before, but I remember it was so good all the children insisted on having one made especially for breakfast for the rest of the holiday, and I still find it a treat for breakfast if I have any left over from the previous day's lunch or supper.

1 large cooking apple　　　　　*100 g (4 oz) sugar*
450 g (1 lb) blackberries　　　*about 8 thin slices white bread*
1.5 dl (¼ pint) water

Peel and core the apple and slice thinly. Put into a saucepan with the blackberries and water, and simmer until tender. Remove from the heat, stir in the sugar and allow to cool. Remove the crusts from the bread. Trim a circle of bread to fit the bottom of a 1.2 litre (2 pint) pudding basin. Line the sides of the basin with fingers of bread, shaped wider at one end than the other, making sure they fit well together. Add a little fruit and juice and then cover with a layer of bread. Continue until the basin is full, finishing with a layer of bread; about 3 layers in all. Cover with a plate which covers the top of the basin, and place a heavy weight on top of that. Leave in the fridge or a cool place for about 8 hours. Turn out and serve with cream. *Serves 4 to 6*

Dinner Parties

I think a dinner party is one of the nicest ways of entertaining as, unlike a buffet or drinks party, when you are usually battling over the noise of everyone else speaking, you actually have the time to sit down and talk to people. However, if you have asked people for 'dinner' rather than 'supper' they do expect something rather better than stewed scrag end of mutton or grilled pork belly rashers, but it is quite possible to present some impressive-looking, and tasting, dishes without having to starve for the rest of the week because you have overspent.

I often feel that the starter is more important than the main course as people are hungry and appreciative at this stage of the meal, so I generally try to give my guests a fairly filling starter, such as a vegetable soup, pâté with plenty of bread, or stuffed pancakes as in the recipe on page 78. I am always very generous with bread at this stage of the meal as, if it is good bread, people eat masses of it which quickly fills them up, and when you serve up the main course, they don't notice that they haven't got a massive portion of meat on their plate! The flavour and presentation of a starter is also important: soups obviously are no problem; if you don't have a large soup tureen you can always use a pretty casserole, and I like to top them with chopped parsley, chives, or other fresh herbs. The Avocado, Celery and Turnip Salad, Leeks Vinaigrette, and Salami and Celeriac Salad are all easy to make and look attractive, and hot starters, such as the Crab Tartlets and Cheese Boreks, can just be garnished with fresh parsley or watercress.

However, before you decide on the starter you must of

course choose your main course as you can't, for example, precede Hare and Prunes with a vegetable soup. One of the chief considerations when choosing a main course (apart from your own obvious likes and dislikes) is how much time you have available for doing the cooking. Do you want to be able to make it the day before and reheat it, in which case a casserole such as Irish Casserole, or Chicken Provençale would be a good choice, or do you want a dish with the minimum amount of preparation and cooking time, such as Liver Stroganoff or Pork with Cranberry? Other dishes, such as Poor Man's Beef Wellington and Lamb Chops in Pastry, can be prepared several hours in advance and then cooked shortly before serving.

When it comes to vegetables I don't usually decide what I am going to serve until I actually go out to do the shopping and see what is available. I have given some ideas for vegetables which are generally cheap, such as Bashed Neeps and Brussels Sprouts with Bacon, but prices vary enormously, not only from year to year and month to month, but also from week to week. Regrettably, just because spinach was cheap last week, it may not be this, as in the intervening few days it may have been hit by frost, flood, drought or other weather conditions, or apparently for no reason at all it can suddenly become scarce and expensive.

Although I prefer serving fresh vegetables you may sometimes find frozen ones are better value, or more convenient if you are short of time, and there are all sorts of ways in which you can make them more interesting. Whether you are using fresh or frozen vegetables it is most important not to overcook them; personally I like them to have a slight crunch to them, and I top them with plenty of freshly milled black pepper, chopped parsley or chives, or a herb butter; thyme, savory (especially for beans), lemon balm, marjoram, etc., can all be finely chopped and added to butter which you can then just put on top of vegetables before serving.

Little new potatoes, boiled or steamed in their skins to retain all their vitamins, are one of the easiest vegetables of all, but other simple, inexpensive vegetables are finely shredded cabbage lightly cooked and sprinkled with some caraway seeds, Jerusalem artichokes topped with fried crumbs as in the recipe for Bashed Neeps, runner beans topped with a spoonful of soured cream, and carrots, lightly steamed or boiled, then fried in a little butter or margarine and topped with a little natural yogurt.

When it comes to the pudding, it is all too easy to get carried away and lash out on masses of cream, booze and fresh fruit. As many puddings are fruit based you obviously want to make them when the fruit is in season, although in most cases you can use frozen fruit which is fairly cheap if you have frozen it yourself. Whilst I have used cream in the Banana and Ginger Cream I have extended it by using yogurt as well, and if you have another favourite recipe for a fruit fool you could try this combination. Rather than using liqueurs, which are a horrific price, I often use white rum, and I frequently use whisky in place of brandy in recipes – whisky butter is just as nice as brandy butter and much easier on the purse. As well as the recipes I have given here, you will also find several in the Buffet Party chapter which are just as suitable for a dinner party, which should give you a fairly wide choice.

One final tip, try to get the meal ready on time as if you have to end up serving another round of drinks because something isn't quite cooked any money you have saved on the food will be completely wasted!

Brussels Sprouts Soup

For this you can use the cheaper, large sprouts, and it is not necessary to trim any but the very outside leaves.

450 g (1 lb) Brussels sprouts
1 medium-sized onion or 1
* leek, chopped*

9 dl (1½ pints) good stock
1.5 dl (¼ pint) single cream
2 rashers streaky bacon

Remove only the very outside leaves of the Brussels sprouts and put into a pan with the onion or leek and stock. Cover, bring to the boil and simmer gently for 45 minutes, or until the sprouts are very tender. Sieve or purée in a blender and return to the pan. Taste and adjust the seasoning and reheat gently. Stir in the cream and heat for 2 to 3 minutes, without allowing the soup to boil. Grill or fry the rashers or bacon until crisp, then crumble them. Turn soup into a soup tureen or serving dish and sprinkle over the crumbled bacon. *Serves 6*

Creamy Cauliflower Soup

As cauliflowers can become very expensive this soup is obviously *not* economical all through the year; however, there are times when you can buy cauliflowers very cheaply, and for soup-making you do not need a perfect white head.

1 medium-sized cauliflower
75 g (3 oz) margarine
1 large onion, peeled and
* chopped*
9 dl (1½ pints) stock
9 dl (1½ pints) milk

a few parsley stalks
1 bay leaf
25 g (1 oz) flour
salt and freshly milled black
* pepper*

Break the cauliflower into florets, discard all the green leaves, but it is not necessary to discard all the central stalk. Heat 50 g (2 oz) of the margarine in a pan, add the onion and cauliflower florets, cover and cook gently for 10 minutes, shaking the pan frequently. Add the stock and milk and bring to the boil. Tie the parsley stalks and bay leaf together with a piece of thread and add to the pan. Cover and simmer gently for 30 minutes or until the cauliflower is very tender. Remove from the heat and sieve or purée in a blender. Melt the remaining margarine in a pan, add the flour and cook for a minute, then gradually stir in the puréed soup. Bring to the boil, stirring all the time. Simmer for 5 minutes, then taste and adjust the seasoning before serving. *Serves 8*

Chilled Summer Soup

I find this a very good way of using up the outside leaves of lettuces. If you wish, you can omit the watercress and use an equivalent amount of lettuce, although the watercress does improve the flavour of the soup.

40 g (1½ oz) butter or margarine
½ lettuce, chopped
1 bunch of watercress, chopped
1 bunch of spring onions, chopped

4.5 dl (¾ pint) milk
4.5 dl (¾ pint) chicken stock
salt and freshly milled black pepper
1.5 dl (¼ pint) natural yogurt

Melt the butter or margarine in a pan. Add the lettuce, watercress and spring onions and cook in a covered pan over a gentle heat for 10 minutes. Add the milk, stock and seasoning. Cover the pan and simmer gently for about 20 minutes or until the vegetables are tender. Remove from the heat and either sieve or purée in a blender. Add the yogurt and whisk well. Turn the soup into a soup tureen or serving dish and chill for at least 4 hours before serving. *Serves 4 to 6*

Salami and Celeriac Salad

This is one of my favourite winter starters; it looks very attractive if you pile the celeriac salad into the centre of a serving dish and arrange the salami round the edge. Salami is, of course, terribly expensive these days, but here one wants to take a tip from the Continentals and make sure they slice the salami as thinly as possible for you at your grocers or delicatessen. On the Continent they literally cut it into wafer thin slices and, provided you insist on it, they will here as well and it is amazing just how many slices there are in 25 g (1 oz) when it is cut this way.

900 g (2 lb) celeriac
little vinegar or lemon juice
salt
3 dl (½ pint) mayonnaise
1 tablespoon chopped parsley
1 teaspoon French mustard
2 teaspoons capers, finely chopped

1 large dill cucumber, finely chopped
freshly milled black pepper
100 to 150 g (4 to 6 oz) salami, very thinly sliced
paprika to garnish

Peel the celeriac and cut into thin matchstick pieces. Since celeriac discolours very quickly, as soon as the pieces have been cut, put them into cold water, acidulated with a little vinegar or lemon juice. Bring a large pan of salted water to the boil, drain the celeriac from the cold water, add to the pan and cook for 1 minute. Remove from the heat, drain well, then rinse quickly in cold water. Dry thoroughly and turn into a bowl. Add all the remaining ingredients and mix well. Pile the celeriac mixture into the centre of a serving dish and arrange the slices of salami around the edge. Cover the dish with cling-wrap and place in the fridge until ready to serve, then sprinkle with a little paprika. *Serves 8*

Crab Tartlets

These may sound very extravagant, but small crabs can often be bought quite cheaply, although they are of course quite fiddly to dress. I like to cook them in individual tartlet tins, but if you do not have any, you can make a whole flan using a 22.5 cm (9 inch) diameter tin. The tartlets can be served cold or warm and they can be made in advance and reheated before serving.

225 g (8 oz) shortcrust pastry (page 187)
1 small crab, 350 g (12 oz) approximately
25 g (1 oz) butter
1 small onion, peeled and very finely chopped
2 eggs, lightly beaten
3 dl (½ pint) single cream or use half cream and half milk
1 tablespoon chopped parsley
salt and freshly milled black pepper
2 tablespoons Parmesan cheese (optional)

Roll out the pastry and use to line 8 x 10 to 12.5cm (4 to 5 inch) tins. Prick the bases lightly with a fork, fill the centres with a circle of greaseproof paper and some baking beans and bake blind in a moderately hot oven, 190°C (375°F), Gas Mark 5 for 8 minutes. Remove the greaseproof paper and beans and bake for a further 5 minutes to dry out the bases. While the pastry is cooking, remove the meat from the crab shell and claws. Melt the butter in a small pan and fry the onion gently for 5 minutes. Beat the eggs, then beat in the cream, parsley and seasoning. Add the onion, crab meat (including the brown meat) and cheese, if using, and mix well. Divide this mixture between the tartlet cases. Bake in a moderate oven, 180°C (350°F), Gas Mark 4, for about 15 minutes or until the filling has set and is golden brown. *Serves 8*

Cheese Boreks

These make an unusual starter. Boreks should be made with filo pastry, but this is difficult and complicated to make and a packet of puff pastry makes a very good substitute. Although they are at their very nicest when first removed from the oven, they can very well be made the day before and reheated in a moderately hot oven for 10 minutes.

For the topping:
100 g (4 oz) curd cheese
a little milk
1½ tablespoons chopped
  chives
1 tablespoon chopped parsley
1 clove of garlic, crushed
salt and freshly milled black
  pepper

For the pastries:
368 g (13 oz) packet frozen
  puff pastry, thawed
225 g (8 oz) Emmenthal,
Jarslburg or Samsoe cheese,
  very thinly sliced

First make the topping, beat the curd cheese with sufficient milk to make a spreading consistency. Beat in the herbs, garlic and seasoning. Cover and chill for a least 1 to 2 hours before serving.

Roll the puff pastry out very thinly and cut out 32 x 7.5 cm (3 inch) circles with a plain cutter. Cut the cheese into as many circles as possible, slightly smaller than the pastry ones, but you will obviously have quite a few trimmings. Place 8 of the pastry circles on a damp baking sheet, cover with a slice of cheese, damp the edges and cover with a second circle of pastry. Repeat these layers so that in each borek you have 4 layers of pastry and 3 of cheese. Brush the tops with a little beaten egg and bake in a very hot oven, 230°C (450°F), Gas Mark 8, for about 10 minutes or until golden brown. Serve each borek hot, topped with a spoonful of the cold cream cheese mixture. *Serves 8*

Leeks Vinaigrette

This makes a very attractive winter starter, particularly if you garnish it with a few chopped or whole black olives. Ideally you should use very small thin leeks, and allow 2 to 3 per person, but if you cannot buy these use large leeks, allow one per person, and slice them in half lengthways after they have been cooked.

12 to 18 small leeks	7 tablespoons oil, preferably olive oil
salt	
1½ teaspoons French mustard	3 tablespoons wine vinegar
	To garnish:
1 clove of garlic, crushed (optional)	2 tablespoons chopped parsley
freshly milled black pepper	about 8 black olives, pitted (optional)

Trim the leeks, removing almost all the green part, and wash very well in cold running water to remove all the mud and grit. Cook the leeks in the very minimum boiling salted water until they are just tender, then drain and dry well with kitchen paper. While the leeks are cooking make a French dressing with the mustard, garlic (if using), pepper, salt, oil and vinegar. Place the leeks in a shallow dish, pour over the dressing while they are still warm and leave for at least 1 hour before serving. Sprinkle with the chopped parsley and garnish with the olives (if wished) before serving. *Serves 6*

Liver and Bacon Pâté

This is an extremely easy and economical pâté. I think it is nicest made with chicken livers, although I have made it very successfully with pig's. I usually try to use bacon trimmings, which you can often buy cheaply.

50 g (2 oz) butter or margarine

225 g (8 oz) chickens' livers or pig's liver

225 g (8 oz) fatty bacon, derinded

1 medium-sized onion, peeled and chopped

1 clove of garlic, crushed

For the sauce:

3 dl (½ pint) milk

1 blade of mace or a good pinch of ground mace

1 bay leaf

4 peppercorns

25 g (1 oz) butter or margarine

25 g (1 oz) flour

1 teaspoon anchovy essence

2 teaspoons made mustard

salt and freshly milled black pepper

Melt the butter or margarine in a frying pan and gently fry the liver, bacon, onion and garlic for about 10 minutes. Remove from the heat and either mince or purée in a blender. While the liver is frying, put the milk into a pan with the mace, bay leaf and peppercorns. Bring slowly to the boil, remove from the heat and leave for 5 minutes. Strain the milk. Melt the remaining butter or margarine in a pan, stir in the flour and cook for a minute. Gradually stir in the strained milk and bring to the boil, stirring all the time until the sauce thickens. Remove from the heat and stir in the meat mixture, anchovy essence and mustard. Season to taste. Turn the mixture into a small, well-greased terrine or meat tin. Cover with foil and/or a lid and stand the terrine or tin in a roasting tin containing 2.5 cm (1 inch) of cold water. Bake in a moderate oven, 180°C (350°F), Gas Mark 4, for 1 hour. Remove from the oven, allow to cool and then chill. The flavour of the pâté will improve if it is kept for a day before eating. If you like to make a really professional finish, you can spoon some melted butter over the top of the pâté to seal it. Serve with hot toast or French or wholemeal bread. *Serves 8*

Avocado, Celery and Turnip Salad

The price of avocados can vary considerably throughout the year, but they are usually at their cheapest in February and March. One tends to think of always serving half an avocado per person with a filling or dressing for a first course, but if you chop them up it is possible to extend one avocado so that it serves 4 people. Turnips are delicious eaten raw, and the contrast in texture between the crisp celery and turnip and the soft avocado is excellent. If you wanted, you could extend this recipe into a light main dish, with one or two other salads, by adding 225 g (8 oz) diced cooked ham, chicken or other cooked meat.

2 ripe avocados
3 tablespoons French dressing
225 g (8 oz) turnips
3 sticks celery, chopped
3 tablespoons thick mayonnaise
2 tablespoons soured cream
a few drops of Tabasco
salt and freshly milled black pepper
a few crisp lettuce leaves
3 rashers streaky bacon

Peel the avocados, cut into 1.5 cm (½ inch) pieces and toss quickly in the French dressing to preserve the colour. Peel the turnips, then cut into 0.75 cm (¼ inch) dice. Add to the avocados with the chopped celery, then stir in the mayonnaise, soured cream and Tabasco. Season to taste with salt and pepper, then arrange on 8 individual plates on crisp lettuce leaves. Grill the bacon until it is crisp, crumble it into small pieces and sprinkle over the top of the salad. *Serves 8*

Mussel Brochettes

The great advantage of this recipe is that, unlike so many other mussel dishes, you can prepare it in advance.

2.5 litres (4 pints) mussels
1 onion, peeled and chopped
1 bay leaf
a few parsley stalks
1.5 dl (¼ pint) water
100 g (4 oz) butter

2 tablespoons chopped parsley
1 tablespoon lemon juice
1 clove of garlic, crushed
about 12 rashers streaky bacon

Put the mussels into a bowl of cold water to soak; this removes some of the excess salt and helps reduce the chore of cleaning them. Scrub the mussels with a brush to remove all traces of seaweed, mud and grit. Discard any which are cracked or are open and do not close when sharply tapped. Put the onion, bay leaf, parsley stalks and water into a large pan and bring to the boil. Add the mussels, cover the pan tightly and cook for about 5 minuts or until all the mussels are open; discard any which do not open. Remove from the heat and take the mussels out of their shells.

Cream the butter and beat in the parsley, lemon juice and garlic. Cut the rind off the bacon and stretch the rashers of bacon with a knife on a board. Spread the bacon with butter, then cut lengths large enough to wrap round the mussels. Wrap a piece of bacon round each mussel and divide between 8 skewers. Just before serving, put under a moderate grill for about 5 minutes, turning once or twice until the bacon is crisp and brown. Place on individual serving plates, pour over the juices from the grill pan and serve with French bread. *Serves 8*

Bacon and Plum Casserole

An unlikely sounding combination but a very good one. Collar and bacon hock are two very good value-for-money joints, but you want to choose them carefully or you may find that they are very fatty. Quite often when I am at the bacon counter in the supermarket I look through the joints and if there is a good lean joint of hock or collar I buy it and freeze it. Although you can't store bacon for too long in the freezer, you can keep it for several weeks, and it is comforting to have a joint like this tucked away.

1.25 kg (3 lb) bacon forehock	25g (1 oz) butter or mar-
2 onions, peeled and chopped	garine
a few black peppercorns	2 sticks celery, chopped
1 small bay leaf	1 tablespoon cornflour
567 g (1 lb 4oz) can Victoria	2 teaspoons made mustard
plums	salt and freshly milled black
	pepper

Soak the bacon for about 4 hours, then drain and put into a large pan. Add one of the onions, the peppercorns and bay leaf and cover with fresh cold water. Bring to the boil, then reduce the heat and simmer very gently for 1 hour. Remove the meat from the cooking liquor, peel or cut off the skin, cut the meat into slices and place in a casserole.

Strain the syrup from the plums, pour it into a measuring jug and make up to 6 dl (1 pint) with the stock from cooking the bacon. Cut the plums in half and remove the stones. Melt the butter or margarine in a pan and gently fry the remaining onion and celery for about 5 minutes. Pour over almost all the syrup and ham stock and bring to the boil. Blend the remaining ham stock with the cornflour in a basin, pour over most of the boiling stock and stir, then return to the heat and bring to the boil, stirring all the time until the sauce thickens. Add the mustard and plums and season to taste with salt and pepper. Pour over the ham, cover and cook in a moderate oven, 180°C (350F), Gas Mark 4, for 1 hour. Taste and adjust the seasoning of the sauce before serving. *Serves 6*

Chicken Provençale

There must be more recipes for Chicken Provençale than almost anything else, and it can become rather monotonous, but this recipe is a particular favourite of mine. If you are feeling extravagant, you can add some saffron to it as well.

1.25 kg (3 lb) chicken
25 g (1 oz) flour
salt and freshly milled black
   pepper
3 tablespoons oil, preferably
   olive oil but you can use
   corn or vegetable
2 onions, peeled and chopped
2 cloves of garlic, crushed

450 g (1 lb) tomatoes, peeled
   and chopped
100 g (4 oz) black olives,
   stoned
1 bouquet garni
3 dl (½ pint) dry white wine
   or cider
juice of 1 lemon
2 tablespoons chopped parsley

Joint the chicken. (I generally cut it into fairly small joints, i.e. wings, half breasts, drumsticks, etc., as two small joints always look much more than one large joint!) Toss the joints in the flour, seasoned with salt and pepper. Heat the oil in a large pan and fry the chicken joints until golden brown all over. Remove from the pan and place in a casserole. Add the onions and garlic to the pan and fry for 5 minutes. Add the tomatoes, olives, bouquet garni and wine or cider and bring to the boil. Pour over the chicken in the casserole. Cover and cook in a moderate oven, 180°C (350°F), Gas Mark 4 for 1 hour or until the chicken is quite tender. Remove the bouquet garni, stir in the lemon juice, then taste and adjust the seasoning. Sprinkle with the parsley before serving.   *Serves 6*

Mackerel with Gooseberry Stuffing

The affinity between mackerel and gooseberries is well known and mackerel with gooseberry sauce is a very famous old English dish. I have suggested using canned gooseberries, as you can buy these throughout the year, but obviously when they are in season you should use freshly stewed gooseberries.

6 mackerel, about 350 g (12 oz) each
50 g (2 oz) margarine
1 medium-sized onion, peeled and very finely chopped
567 g (1 lb 4 oz) can gooseberries
grated rind and juice of 1 small lemon

150 g (6 oz) fresh brown breadcrumbs
¼ teaspoon dried tarragon
salt and freshly milled black pepper
1.5 dl (¼ pint) water
To garnish:
1 lemon, sliced

Clean the fish, leaving the heads and tails in place, or ask the fishmonger to do this for you. Melt the margarine in a small pan and gently fry the onion for 5 minutes. Remove from the heat. Strain the juice from the gooseberries and reserve. Chop two-thirds of the gooseberries fairly finely and put into a basin with the onion, lemon rind, breadcrumbs, tarragon and seasoning. Mix well, then divide this stuffing between the stomach cavities of the fish. Place the fish in an ovenproof dish and season well with salt and pepper. Mix the lemon juice with the water and 1.5 dl (¼ pint) of the reserved gooseberry syrup, then pour over the fish. Cover with foil or a lid and bake in a moderately hot oven 190°C (375°F), Gas Mark 5 for 30 minutes. Remove from the oven, place on a serving dish and garnish with the remaining gooseberries and the sliced lemon. *Serves 6*

Roast Pork with Orange Stuffing

A hand of pork is usually a good buy; choose it carefully though, or you may find it is very fatty. Stuffing a joint not only makes it more economical, but improves the flavour of the meat and turns it into something rather more 'special'.

a hand of pork, about 2.25 kg
  (5 lb)
150 g (6 oz) fresh white
  breadcrumbs
50 g (2 oz) margarine, melted
grated rind of 1 orange
1 medium-sized onion, peeled
  and finely chopped or
  minced
½ teaspoon dried tarragon
1 medium-sized apple,
  peeled, cored and grated

salt and freshly milled black
  pepper
1 egg, beaten
25 g (1 oz) lard

For the sauce:
1 tablespoon flour
1 orange
4.5 dl (¾ pint) meat or vegetable stock
2 tablespoons sweet sherry or
  port

Score the rind of the pork, if this has not been done already.
Using a sharp knife, cut all round the joint to the bone, parallel to the skin and about 2.5 cm (1 inch) below it. Mix
together the breadcrumbs, margarine, orange rind, onion, tarragon, apple and seasoning and bind the mixture with the
beaten egg. Press the stuffing into the pork, then sew up using
fine string or coarse thread. Spread the lard over the rind of
the pork and season with salt and pepper. Put into a hot oven
220°C (425°F), Gas Mark 7, for 30 minutes, then lower the
heat to 190°C (375°F), Gas Mark 5 and cook for a further 1¾
hours. Remove the pork and place on a heated serving dish.
Should you find that for some reason the pork has failed to
crackle (this can be caused by excess steam in the oven from
roasting potatoes), do not despair but put the joint under a
moderately hot grill for about 5 minutes to crisp up the crack-
ling.

Drain off all but 1 tablespoon of the fat in the roasting tin,
stir in the flour and put over a low heat on top of the cooker,
stirring frequently until the flour is pale golden brown. Cut off
all the white pith from the orange, then, holding the fruit over
a basin, cut between the skin into segments. Finally squeeze
all the juice out of the skin and pith remaining. Gradually stir
the stock into the roux in the roasting tin. Bring to the boil,
stirring all the time, then add the orange, together with any
juice, and the sherry or port. Taste and adjust the seasoning
and serve this sauce separately with the pork.   Serves 8

Paupiettes of Liver

With the meat for making veal and beef paupiettes becoming more and more expensive, this seems to be a very good alternative – a rather upmarket liver and bacon!

450 g (1 lb) lamb's liver
12 rashers streaky bacon
25 g (1 oz) butter or margarine
1 small onion, peeled and
grated
100 g (4 oz) fresh white
breadcrumbs
1 clove of garlic, crushed
1 small cooking apple,
peeled, cored and grated

salt and freshly milled black
pepper
2 tablespoons chopped parsley
2 tablespoons vegetable oil
1 large onion, peeled and
chopped
400 g (14 oz) can tomatoes
1 tablespoon tomato purée
1.5 dl (¼ pint) water
3 sage leaves

Cut the liver into 12 thin slices. Cut off the rind from the bacon and stretch each rasher with the back of a knife. Melt the butter or margarine in a small pan and gently fry the small onion for 5 minutes. Stir in the breadcrumbs, garlic, apple, seasoning and parsley and mix well. Divide the stuffing between the 12 slices of liver. Roll up each one carefully, then wrap a rasher of bacon round each. Tie in place with thread or fine string. Heat the oil in a pan and quickly fry the rolls on all sides. Remove from the pan and put on one side. Add the large onion and fry gently for 5 minutes, then add the tomatoes, together with the juice from the can, tomato purée, water, sage and seasoning. Replace the rolls. Cover the pan and simmer very gently for 45 minutes. Taste and adjust the seasoning before serving.   *Serves 6*

Lamb Cutlets in Pastry

A solitary lamb cutlet, even if it is of a reasonable size, looks a pretty mean helping on a plate, but if you wrap it in pastry with a small amount of stuffing, it immediately takes on an entirely different aspect and becomes quite generous.

8 large lamb cutlets
salt and freshly milled black
  pepper
1 or 2 sprigs of rosemary
25 g (1 oz) butter or margarine
1 large onion, peeled and very
  finely chopped
100 g (4 oz) mushrooms,
  finely chopped

3 lambs' kidneys, skinned,
  cored and finely chopped
2 tablespoons chopped parsley
350 g (12 oz) puff pastry
  (page 188) or 1 x 368 g (13
  oz) and a 210 g (8 oz) packet frozen puff pastry,
  thawed
1 egg yolk
2 tablespoons water

Season the cutlets with salt and pepper and place on a grill
pan with the rosemary. Grill on both sides until they are just
tender, about 10 minutes. Remove from the heat and allow to
cool. Melt the butter or margarine in a pan and gently fry the
onion for 5 minutes. Add the mushrooms and fry for a further
5 minutes, then add the kidneys and cook for a further 5
minutes. Stir in the parsley and season to taste. Roll the pastry
out thinly and cut out 8 pieces large enough to cover the
cutlets completely. Beat the egg yolk with the water and brush
the edges of the pastry. Put a spoonful of the stuffing in the
centre of each piece of pastry and place a chop on top. Fold
the pastry over and seal the edges, so that each cutlet is completely enclosed in the pastry. Place on a baking sheet with
the joins underneath. Roll out the trimmings, cut into leaves
for decoration and place in position. Brush all over the top of
the pastry with the beaten egg and bake in a hot oven, 220°C
(425°F), Gas Mark 7, for about 20 minutes or until golden
brown. *Serves 8*

Liver Stroganoff

This is a good dinner party dish when you are short of time as
there is very little preparation involved and the total cooking
time is only about 12 minutes. Liver makes an excellent and
cheap alternative to the fillet steak or good quality rump,
which is used in the well-known Russian dish, Beef
Stroganoff.

500 g (1 ¼ lb) liver
salt and freshly milled black
  pepper
75 g (3 oz) butter
1 large onion, peeled and
  finely chopped

150 g (6 oz) mushrooms,
  finely chopped
2 tablespoons tomato purée
3 tablespoons dry sherry
a pinch of dried thyme
3 dl (½ pint) soured cream

Cut the liver into thin strips about 0.75 cm (¼ inch) thick, and 5 cm (2 inches) long and season with salt and pepper. Melt the butter in a large frying pan and gently fry the onion and mushrooms for 5 minutes. Add the liver and cook, stirring, for a further 2 to 3 minutes, then add the tomato purée, sherry and thyme, and cook for a further 2 to 3 minutes. Stir in the cream and heat gently, without allowing the mixture to boil. Taste, adjust the seasoning and serve with boiled rice, new potatoes or boiled noodles.   *Serves 6*

Poor Man's Beef Wellington

Beef Wellington should, of course, be made with fillet steak, but as this is now beyond the reach of most of our purses, I find this version using minced beef extremely popular. You must, however, use good quality minced beef.

900 g (2 lb) minced beef
1 medium-sized onion, peeled
  and finely chopped
2 cloves of garlic, crushed
2 egg yolks
1 tablespoon Worcestershire
  sauce
1 tablespoon made mustard
salt and freshly milled black
  pepper

2 tablespoons oil
225 g (8 oz) good quality
  liver sausage
225 g (8 oz) puff pastry (page
  188) or use a 368 g (13 oz)
  packet frozen puff pastry,
  thawed
egg to glaze

Put the minced beef into a basin and add the onion, garlic, egg yolks, Worcestershire sauce, mustard and seasoning. Mix well, then form into a roll approximately 22.5 cm (9 inches) long. Heat the oil in a pan and fry the meat quickly until it is browned on all sides. Remove from the pan and allow to cool. Roll out the pastry to a rectangle large enough to completely envelop the meat. Spread with the liver sausage to within 2.5 cm (1 inch) of the edges. Place the meat roll in the centre. Brush the edges of the pastry with beaten egg and bring them together to completely enclose the meat. Place on a baking sheet with the joins underneath. Roll out the pastry trimmings and cut into leaves. Brush with egg and place in position on the top of the pastry. Brush all over the pastry with beaten egg. Bake in a hot oven, 220°C (425°F), Gas Mark 7, for 30 to 40 minutes or until the pastry is golden brown.   *Serves 8*

Irish Casserole

This rich casserole is made with that marvellous Irish product – Guinness – and the flavour will in fact improve if it is made the day before and then reheated.

900 g (2 lb) stewing steak	4.5 dl (¾ pint) water
25 g (1 oz) lard or dripping	1 teaspoon dried thyme or 2
3 large onions, peeled and	sprigs fresh thyme
chopped	1 teaspoon sugar
40 g (1½ oz) flour	salt and freshly milled black
4.5 dl (¾ pint) Guinness	pepper

Cut the beef into 4 cm (1½ inch) cubes. Heat the lard or dripping in a flameproof casserole and fry the meat until it is browned on all sides. Remove from the pan with a draining spoon and put on one side. Add the onions to the pan and fry gently until golden. Stir in the flour and cook for 2 minutes, stirring. Gradually stir in the Guinness and water and bring to the boil, stirring all the time. Add the thyme, sugar and seasoning. Replace the meat in the casserole, cover and cook in a very moderate oven, 170°C (325°F), Gas Mark 3, for about 2 hours or until the meat is tender. Taste and adjust the seasoning before serving.   *Serves 6*

Casseroled Hare with Walnuts and Prunes

A hare may sound very extravagant, but in fact a large hare will serve 8 people comfortably, and works out at about the same price as stewing steak.

For the marinade:
3 dl (½ pint) dry cider
1 onion, peeled and chopped
6 juniper berries, crushed
2 cloves of garlic, crushed
thinly peeled rind and juice of
  1 lemon
1 sprig of thyme
salt and freshly milled black
  pepper

For the hare:
1 large hare
100 g (4 oz) prunes
3 dl (½ pint) water
225 g (8 oz) bacon pieces
2 tablespoons oil
2 large onions, peeled and
  chopped
25 g (1 oz) flour
3 dl (½ pint) stock
50 g (2 oz) walnut pieces

Put all the ingredients for the marinade into a pan and bring to the boil. Simmer gently for 5 minutes, then remove from the heat and allow to cool. Joint the hare and place in a shallow dish, pour over the marinade and leave for at least 6 hours. Meanwhile, soak the prunes in the water. Remove the hare from the marinade, dry it and strain the marinade.

Chop the bacon roughly, put it into a large flameproof casserole and cook gently for about 8 minutes or until the fat is running. Add the pieces of hare and cook on all sides until browned. Remove the hare and bacon from the pan and put on one side. Add the oil to the pan, heat it, add the onion and cook gently for 5 minutes. Stir in the flour and cook gently for 2 to 3 minutes, stirring all the time. Gradually add in the stock and the strained marinade and bring to the boil, stirring constantly. Replace the hare and bacon pieces, add the prunes, together with the liquor in which they have been soaking, cover the casserole and cook in a very moderate oven, 170°C (325°F), Gas Mark 3, for 2 to 2½ hours. Pound or grind the walnuts until smooth. Stir into the sauce just before serving, taste and adjust the seasoning. *Serves 8*

Devilled Kidneys

There is almost no waste at all in a kidney, other than the small amount of core, which makes them a very good buy. I like the flavour of pig's kidneys, which are cheaper than lamb's, but if you find it a bit too strong, soak them in a little milk for an hour before cooking.

6 large pig's kidneys
50 g (2 oz) flour
salt and freshly milled black
   pepper
50 g (2 oz) lard or dripping
2 large onions, peeled and
   sliced
1 red pepper, seeded and
   chopped (optional)
227 g (8 oz) can tomatoes

3 dl (½ pint) stock
1 tablespoon made English
   mustard
1 tablespoon Worcestershire
   sauce
To garnish:
4 rashers streaky bacon
1 tablespoon chopped parsley.

Cut the kidneys into slices, discarding the cores, and toss in the flour, seasoned with salt and pepper. Heat the lard or dripping in a large pan and fry the onions and pepper (if using) for 5 minutes. Add the kidneys and fry for a further 5 minutes, stirring frequently. Stir in any excess flour, then stir in the tomatoes, together with the juice from the can, the stock, mustard and Worcestershire sauce and bring to the boil, stirring all the time. Cover the pan and simmer gently for 20 minutes or until the kidneys are quite tender. Taste and adjust the seasoning. Grill the bacon rashers until crisp, then chop finely. Turn the kidneys into a heated serving dish, and sprinkle with the chopped bacon and parsley. *Serves 6*

Pork Spareribs with Cranberry Sauce

I find sparerib chops very good value for money; they are considerably cheaper than loin chops, and although there is some fat on them, it is mostly integrated with the lean which makes it very palatable and keeps the lean moist.

6 sparerib pork chops	1.5 dl (¼ pint) stock
salt and freshly milled black pepper	185 g (6.5 oz) jar cranberry sauce
1 tablespoon oil	½ teaspoon ground ginger
2 medium-sized onions, peeled and finely chopped	To garnish: watercress

Season the chops well with salt and pepper. Heat the oil in a large frying pan and quickly fry the chops until they are browned on both sides. Remove from the pan and put on one side. Add the onions to the fat remaining in the pan and fry gently for 5 minutes. Pour over the stock and add the cranberry sauce and ginger. Replace the chops in the pan and bring to the boil. Cover the pan and simmer gently for 20 minutes, then taste and adjust the seasoning. Turn onto a heated serving dish and garnish with watercress. *Serves 6*

Stewed Leeks with Lemon

I am a great fan of the leek, and they are generally one of the cheaper vegetables. They are excellent boiled or steamed and served in a white sauce, but this can be rather a bother when you are entertaining and have several other last-minute things to do. Cooked this way they require very little last-minute attention and taste extremely good.

900 g (2 lb) leeks	salt
50 g (2 oz) butter or margarine	1 tablespoon lemon juice
	freshly milled black pepper

Cut the leeks into 1.5 cm (½ inch) slices and wash thoroughly. Dry well. Melt the butter or margarine in a pan or frying pan. Add the leeks, together with the salt, cover the pan and simmer very gently for about 20 minutes. They must cook over a gentle heat, and be stirred from time to time or they may burn. Pour over the lemon juice and season to taste with plenty of freshly milled black pepper. *Serves 6*

Poor Man's Ratatouille

Ratatouille is a very good dinner party dish as you can make it in advance and reheat it in the oven or on top of the stove, which saves a lot of last-minute fuss preparing fresh vegetables, as I really do like to cook my green vegetables just before I serve them. Obviously there are times of the year when it is extremely expensive to make, but recently I have found that the price of aubergines and peppers has not increased as much as some of the other less exotic vegetables and so they are generally quite good value for money. I have used canned tomatoes here as they are generally cheaper, but in their peak season fresh ones can work out cheaper, especially if you are growing them yourself. The proportion of courgettes in this version is also slightly high as they are generally the cheapest ingredient and during the winter you could use frozen ones. Remember that any left over is also excellent served cold as a salad.

1 aubergine, weighing approx 225 g (8 oz)
450 g (1 lb) courgettes
1 teaspoon salt
2 tablespoons oil
2 large onions, peeled and sliced
2 cloves of garlic, crushed
1 red pepper, seeded and sliced

1 green pepper, seeded and sliced
567 g (1 lb 4 oz) can tomatoes
1 teaspoon coriander seeds, crushed
a sprig of fresh thyme
freshly milled black pepper

Cut the aubergine and courgettes into 1.5 cm (½ inch) pieces. Place in a colander, sprinkle with the salt and leave to drain for 30 minutes. Heat the oil in a pan and gently fry the onions and garlic for 5 minutes. Add the peppers, courgettes and aubergines and cook for a further 10 minutes. Add the tomatoes, together with the juice from the can, and the coriander, thyme and seasoning. Cover the pan and simmer gently for 30 minutes. Taste and adjust the seasoning before serving. *Serves 8 to 10*

Stovie Potatoes

This is one of my favourite ways of cooking potatoes for dinner parties as you can just put it in the oven and forget about it. If you are cooking a casserole at a lower temperature, just put the potatoes in the oven with it and increase the cooking time by 30 minutes.

1.2 kg (3 lb) potatoes
450 g (1 lb) onions
salt and freshly milled black
* pepper*

3 dl (½ pint) milk
25 g (1 oz) butter or mar-
* garine*

Peel the potatoes and cut into 0.75 cm (¼ inch) slices. Peel the onions and cut into thin rings. Put a layer of potatoes into a large, ovenproof dish, season with salt and pepper and cover with a layer of onions. Repeat these layers, ending with a layer of potatoes, and seasoning each layer with salt and pepper. Pour over the milk. Dot the top with butter or margarine and cover with a lid or foil. Bake in a moderately hot oven, 190°C (375°F), Gas Mark 5, for about 1½ hours, removing the lid for the last 20 minutes of cooking so that the potatoes can brown on the top. *Serves 8*

Potato and Celeriac Purée

I find celeriac a marvellous winter vegetable. It can be served as a purée just on its own, but the flavour is rather strong and I prefer to mix it with creamed potato.

900 g (2 lb) celeriac
little vinegar or lemon juice
* (see method)*
450 g (1 lb) potatoes
salt

50 g (2 oz) butter or mar-
* garine*
freshly milled black pepper
2 tablespoons chopped pars-
* ley*

Peel the celeriac, cut into even-sized pieces about 5 cm (2 inches) square, and put immediately into water with a little vinegar or lemon juice to preserve the colour. Peel the potatoes and cut into pieces the same size as the celeriac. Bring a pan of salted water to the boil, add the celeriac and potato pieces and cook gently for about 15 minutes or until both the vegetables are quite tender. Remove from the heat and drain very well, then mash with a vegetable masher or put through a ricer or vegetable mill. Beat in the butter or margarine and season to taste with salt and plenty of pepper. Turn into a heated serving dish and sprinkle with the chopped parsley before serving. *Serves 6 to 8*

Bashed Neeps

The poor old swede is a much-maligned vegetable, and if properly cooked can be quite delicious. I have topped it here with crisply fried breadcrumbs and you can make these earlier on in the day and just reheat them in the oven for a short time before serving. If you have a steamer I think that it is much nicer to steam the swede which reduces any risk of it becoming watery, but if boiling, make sure you do not overcook it and press it down in the colander to really squeeze out all the water.

900 g (2 lb) swedes
salt
1 sprig of thyme
75 g (3 oz) butter or margarine

2 tablespoons single cream
¼ teaspoon grated nutmeg
freshly milled black pepper
50 g (2 oz) fresh white or brown breadcrumbs

Peel the swede and cut into 5 cm (2 inch) chunks. Either steam or cook in boiling salted water with the thyme until just tender. Drain very well, then mash with half the butter or margarine and the cream. Add the nutmeg and season to taste with salt and lashings of freshly milled black pepper. Pile into a heated serving dish. Melt the remaining butter or margarine in a frying pan and fry the crumbs until they are crisp and golden brown. Sprinkle over the swede just before serving, so that they do not become soggy. *Serves 6*

Brussels Sprouts with Bacon

This is not a great deal of trouble to prepare, but makes that eternal winter stand-by vegetable, the Brussels sprout, into something just a bit more special.

650 g (1½ lb) Brussels sprouts
salt
100 g (4 oz) fat bacon or bacon trimmings

1 medium-sized onion, peeled and finely chopped
2 tablespoons wine vinegar
freshly milled black pepper

Trim the sprouts and boil them in salted water, or steam them until they are just tender; do not overcook. Drain well and place in a heated serving dish. Put the bacon into a small pan over a low heat and fry until crisp. Remove from the pan and crumble. Add the onion to the fat remaining in the pan and fry gently for 5 minutes. Add the vinegar to the onion in the pan, spoon over the sprouts, season very well with pepper and toss lightly together. Sprinkle over the crumbled bacon just before serving. *Serves 6*

Gooseberry Ice Cream

I love gooseberry fool and gooseberry ice cream, but all the cream tends to make it rather expensive. I experimented making it with a packet of synthetic cream topping and found it was very successful as the tartness of the gooseberries counteracts the sweetness of the mix.

450 g (1 lb) gooseberries
4 tablespoons water
a sprig of mint (optional)
75 g (3 oz) sugar

a little green colouring
1.5 dl (¼ pint) packet synthetic cream topping

Top and tail the gooseberries, put them in a pan with the water and mint (if used). Cover and simmer gently for about 10 minutes or until soft. Remove from the heat, stir in the sugar, then sieve or purée in a blender. Add a little green colouring and allow to cool. Make up the topping according to the instructions on the packet, then fold into the gooseberry purée. Turn into 6 small ramekin dishes and freeze for at least 2 hours. If you want to store the ice cream in the freezer, remove it at least 15 minutes before serving, so that it can soften slightly. *Serves 6*

Banana and Ginger Cream

I sometimes find I have a couple of pieces of stem ginger left in the bottom of a jar, or a slightly mangled half packet of cystallized ginger lurking in the back of the cupboard, and this is a good way of using it up. If you are lucky you can some-times pick up slightly over-ripe or loose bananas quite cheaply and they are perfectly adequate for this. I prefer the recipe made with half yogurt and half cream, but for greater economy you can use all yogurt.

4 large ripe bananas	*50 g (2 oz) stem or cystallized*
3 tablespoons lemon juice	*ginger*
¼ teaspoon ground ginger	*1.5 dl (¼ pint) yogurt*
100 g (4 oz) sugar	*1.5 dl (¼ pint) double cream, lightly whipped*

Peel the bananas and mash with a fork. Stir in the lemon juice, ground ginger, sugar, most of the chopped ginger, reserving a little for sprinkling on the top, and the yogurt. Fold in the whipped cream and turn into a serving dish, or small individual dishes. Chill for 1 hour before serving, but do not prepare this dessert too long before serving as even with the addition of lemon juice the top will start to turn brown. Sprinkle with the reserved pieces of ginger before serving. *Serves 6*

Crêpes Suzette

Crêpes Suzette always sound (and taste) very luxurious, but in fact they are not that expensive. The pancakes themselves are very cheap; the batter I have given here is a very basic one, and if you like you could make it slightly richer by reducing the amount of milk and adding an extra egg and 25 g (1 oz) of melted butter, and they can be made up the day before and simply heated in the orange sauce. Although you should use Cointreau, Curaçao, or Grand Marnier and brandy, I have made some delicious ones using only the remains of a bottle of white rum that I found at the back of the cupboard, and you could use vodka or Marc just as well. If you are really flat broke you can omit all the booze and just serve them in the orange sauce.

For the batter:
100 g (4 oz) plain flour
pinch of salt
1 egg
3 dl (½ pint) milk

For the sauce:
75 g (3 oz) butter, preferably
   unsalted, or margarine
100 g (4 oz) sugar
grated rind and juice 1 large
   orange
2 tablespoons Cointreau,
   Curaçao or Grand Marnier
2 tablespoons brandy or rum

Sift the flour and salt into a bowl. Add the egg and half the milk and beat to a thick, smooth batter. Beat in the remaining milk. Heat a little lard or oil in the pan and use the batter to make 10 to 12 small thin pancakes. Separate each pancake with a sheet of greaseproof paper and wrap in a piece of foil until required. Heat the butter, sugar, orange rind and juice in a large frying pan. Add the Cointreau, Curaçao or Grand Marnier. Fold each pancake into four. Put them into the pan and heat through gently in the sauce, turning them over once. Warm the brandy, pour over the pancakes, quickly set fire to them and serve at once. *Serves 6*

Blackberry Ice Cream

You can use either fresh or frozen blackberries for this super-simple ice cream.

450 g (1 lb) blackberries   *100 g (4 oz) icing sugar,*
3 eggs, separated   *sifted*

Pick over the blackberries and wash them thoroughly under cold water. Drain and put into a heavy-based pan. Cover and cook very slowly for about 10 minutes or until the blackberries are tender. Remove from the heat, sieve, or purée first in a blender and then sieve to remove all the pips. Whisk the egg yolks with just under half the sugar until they are thick and creamy. Stiffly whisk the egg whites, then gradually beat in the remaining icing sugar a teaspoon at a time. Very gradually whisk in the egg yolks and then fold in the blackberry purée. Taste and add a little extra sifted icing sugar if necessary. Turn into a plastic container and freeze for about 1 hour. Remove from the freezer when the ice cream is beginning to harden and beat well, then return to the freezer until the mixture is firm.   *Serves 6 to 8*

Cranberry and Orange Meringue

Cranberries are in season from the end of October until about the middle of February and apart from being used for the inevitable cranberry sauce with roast turkey, they can be used to make delicious puddings.

450 g (1 lb) cranberries   *275 g (10 oz) caster sugar*
grated rind and juice of 1   *3 egg whites*
  large orange

Put the cranberries into a pan with the orange rind and juice and 100 g (4 oz) of the sugar. Cover and simmer very gently for 10 minutes or until the cranberries are quite tender. Turn into an ovenproof dish. Whisk the egg whites until they form stiff peaks, then gradually beat in the remaining sugar, a teaspoon at a time. Pile the meringue on top of the cranberries, then bake in a moderately hot oven 190°C (375°F), Gas Mark 5 for 20 minutes or until the meringue is golden brown. Serve hot or cold with cream.   *Serves 6 to 8*

Blackcurrant Sorbet

Sorbets make a delicious end to the meal and are comparatively inexpensive as they only consist of a fruit purée and sugar syrup, and for this recipe you can use either fresh or frozen blackcurrants. I like to add a couple of whisked egg whites as well as this lightens the texture and also makes them 'go further'.

225 g (8 oz) blackcurrants *225 g (8 oz) sugar*
3 dl (½ pint) water *2 egg whites*
peeled rind of 1 lemon

Put the blackcurrants into a pan with half the water and the lemon rind. Cover the pan and simmer gently for about 20 minutes or until the blackcurrants are tender. Remove from the heat and either purée in a blender and then sieve to remove all the pips, or sieve only.

Put the sugar and remaining water into a clean pan and put over a gentle heat until the sugar has dissolved. Increase the heat, bring the mixture to the boil and boil rapidly for 3 to 4 minutes until the mixture is syrupy. Remove from the heat and pour over the blackcurrants. Mix well and put on one side until cool. Turn into a suitable container for freezing, cover and freeze. When the mixture is half-frozen, remove from the freezer and beat very well until smooth. Whisk the egg whites until they form soft peaks, then fold in. Re-cover, return to the freezer and freeze until firm. Serve with small crisp biscuits.   *Serves 4 to 6*

Normandy Apple Tart

Although this classic French pastry has almost exactly the same ingredients as a homely apple pie, the presentation of it immediately makes people think that they are eating something very special (which they are!).

150 g (6 oz) shortcrust pastry
   (page 187)
900 g (2 lb) cooking apples
3 tablespoons water

100 g (4 oz) sugar
1 tablespoon lemon juice
2 to 3 tablespoons apricot jam

Roll out the pastry and use to line a flan ring or tin 20 to 22. 5 cm (8 to 9 inches) in diameter. Prick the base with a fork, cover the base with greaseproof paper and fill with baking beans. Bake in a moderately hot oven, 190°C (375°F), Gas Mark 5, for about 15 minutes. Remove the paper and beans and bake for a further 5 minutes to dry out the base.

Peel, core and slice 650 g (1½ lb) of the apples. Put into a saucepan with the water and sugar and cook until soft. Remove from the heat, mash with a fork to give a smooth purée, then spoon into the flan case. Peel and core the remaining apples and slice neatly. Arrange these in a circle on top of the apple purée and brush them with lemon juice. Bake in a moderately hot oven for about 25 minutes. Sieve the apricot jam into a small saucepan and heat gently. Remove the flan from the oven and brush all over the top with the warm jam. Serve either warm or cold.   *Serves 6*

Steamed Tutti Frutti Pudding

The first time I ever served this pudding at a dinner party there was a look of horror on all my guests' faces that I should dare to serve such a humble pudding to them at dinner. They all said they only wanted a very small helping, but having tasted it, declared it was the most delicious pudding ever and at the end there wasn't a scrap left on the table!

50 g (2 oz) tenderized prunes
50 g (2 oz) glacé cherries
75 g (3 oz) dried apricots
100 g (4 oz) butter or mar-
garine
100 g (4 oz) caster sugar
grated rind and juice of 1
orange

2 eggs, beaten
75 g (3 oz) self-raising flour
50 g (2 oz) fresh white bread-
crumbs
25 g (1 oz) chopped candied
peel
2 level tablespoons golden
syrup

Chop the prunes, cherries and apricots, reserving 6 apricots for decoration. Cream the butter or margarine and sugar until light and fluffy, then beat in the orange rind. Gradually beat in the eggs, adding a tablespoon of flour with the last amount of egg. Sift the flour and fold in, then fold in the breadcrumbs, chopped prunes, cherries, apricots and the peel. Fold in the orange juice. Grease a 9 dl (1½ pint) pudding basin well and spoon the syrup into the bottom. Arrange the reserved apricots over the syrup, then spoon in the mixture. Cover with a double layer of foil, and steam, either in a steamer or in a saucepan of hot water for 2 hours. Remove from the pan, invert the pudding basin on to a heated serving plate and serve with cream. *Serves 6*

Buffet Parties

Buffet parties are the ideal way of entertaining a number of people for either lunch or supper. Few of us can get more than eight or ten people round our dining room or kitchen tables, so if we want to have more than this number, it inevitably means serving buffet-type food. As far as I am concerned the most essential point about food for a buffet party is that it *must* be easy to eat. If you are not having too many people, it is usually possible to ensure that everyone has a chair, but once you are over a certain number, you cannot be sure of this, and even in a chair I have difficulty trying to cut a piece of meat with two hands, while holding on to a drink with the third. All the recipes in this chapter have therefore been carefully chosen, so that they are easy to eat with either just a fork, or with only a very little help from a knife.

A few years ago, chicken was all the rage at every party one went to, but this now seems to have been replaced by pâtés, terrines and the inevitable savoury flans. Whilst I don't really like serving the same food as everyone else, I enjoy making, and eating, terrines and flans, as you can vary them in so many ways and, provided you choose your ingredients carefully, they are generally very cheap, and are practical for making in large numbers. The pretty china flan dishes one can now buy in every kitchen equipment shop always look attractive, and if you want to make several large flans you can usually find a few friends who are prepared to lend you theirs for a party. You can also use ordinary metal tins and rings, from which it is fairly easy to remove the cooked flan; the easiest way to do this out of a flan tin, is to bake the case blind, allow it to cool, then turn it upside down carefully, so that the case comes out of the tin. You can then fill and bake it in the usual way.

Generally speaking cold buffets are considerably easier than hot ones, as you can prepare so much of the food in advance and there are no last-minute panics. You can put all the food out an hour or so before serving, preferably covered with some cling-wrap (and remember to shut the doors if you have animals), and all you will have to do at the last minute is to toss the odd salad. Equally, it is quite nice sometimes to serve a hot dish, provided you can prepare it well in advance and you do not have to do too much just before serving. I would always avoid serving vegetables, other than baked potatoes in their jackets or boiled rice, as these inevitably require some last-minute attention. Anyway, most people enjoy eating a green salad with their meal, which is much simpler than cooking and preparing vegetables.

If it is a large party, it is usually much easier not to have a starter, as no matter how well organized one tries to be there is usually a queue for food, and this just makes one extra queue; but for smaller parties, Smoked Mackerel Pâté and Hummus are two good starters. It is usually best to have two or three main-course dishes situated in different places, together with salads and accompaniments, so that you don't have everyone converging on the same place at the same time.

If you are not serving a savoury flan for a main course, sweet flans make good desserts, as you can pre-slice them so that they are easy to serve and eat. Mousses also make good puddings for this reason, provided you have plenty of large serving dishes. One of my favourite buffet desserts is the meringue cake; a rather more extravagant meringue pudding I made one day, because the meringue cake I had made broke into countless pieces, was layers of meringue, canned chestnut purée mixed with whipped cream and grated chocolate, finishing with a few swirls of the meringue which had remained intact. This can be varied in many ways: you could layer it up with a fruit purée, such as apple or apricot – or just with fresh fruit, such as raspberries or strawberries, and with preferably some whipped cream in between two of the layers.

Hummus

Hummus makes a good starter for a buffet party, as it is easy for people to eat standing up, with a piece of pitta. I have also served it very successfully as a dip with crudités.

225 g (8 oz) chick peas
salt
juice of 1 lemon
2 cloves of garlic, crushed
1.5 dl (¼ pint) tahina

2 tablespoons chopped parsley
freshly milled black pepper
2 tablespoons oil

Soak the chick peas overnight in cold water. Drain, put into a pan and cover with fresh cold water. Add 1 teaspoon salt, cover, bring to the boil and simmer gently for 2 hours or until the peas are very tender. Drain, reserving the cooking liquor, and sieve or purée in a blender. Add the lemon juice, garlic, tahina and enough of the cooking liquor to make a smooth paste. Add half the parsley and season to taste with salt and pepper. Turn into a serving dish, pour over the oil and sprinkle with the remaining chopped parsley before serving. Serve with pitta bread. *Serves 10*
Note: Tahina is sesame seeds ground to a smooth purée, which can be bought in delicatessens and health food stores.

Smoked Mackerel Pâté

I always find this very popular and it is incredibly easy to make. I prefer to use whole mackerel, rather than fillets, as it is not difficult to skin and bone them, and the one time I used fillets I had a terrible job trying to remove a mass of little bones which had been left in.

2 large smoked mackerel
225 g (8 oz) butter, softened
225 g (8 oz) curd cheese
juice of 1 lemon
1 clove of garlic, crushed

salt and freshly milled black pepper
2 teaspoons dried dill (optional)

Skin and bone the mackerel and flake finely or put into a liquidizer. Beat in the butter, curd cheese, lemon juice and garlic. Season with plenty of pepper, and a little salt, if necessary, and add the dill (if using). Turn into one large or two smaller serving dishes and chill for at least 2 hours before serving. *Serves 10 to 12*

Curried Meat Balls in Cream Sauce

Meat balls are extremely popular in Scandinavia which is where this recipe originated. You can make it the day before a party and reheat, provided you do not add the cream until just before serving.

For the meat balls:
50 g (2 oz) butter or mar-
  garine
450 g (1 lb) onions, peeled
  and grated
1 kg (2¼ lb) lean minced veal
  or pork
1½ teaspoons ground ginger
1 tablespoon curry powder
salt and freshly milled black
  pepper
150 g (6 oz) fresh white
  breadcrumbs
2 eggs, beaten
1.5 dl (¼ pint) single cream

For the sauce:
125 g (5 oz) butter or mar-
  garine
75 g (3 oz) flour
1 tablespoon curry powder
1.2 litres (2 pints) stock
2 tablespoons mango chutney
juice of 1 lemon
salt and freshly milled black
  pepper
3 dl (½ pint) single cream

Melt the butter or margarine for the meat balls in a small pan and cook the onions gently for 5 minutes. Turn into a bowl and add the veal or pork, ginger, curry powder, seasoning and breadcrumbs. Mix together then bind the mixture with the eggs and cream. Beat well, then put into the fridge for about 1 hour until the mixture stiffens slightly. Lightly flour your hands and form the mixture into balls, about the size of a walnut.

Melt the butter or margarine for the sauce in a large frying pan and fry the meat balls, in batches, until golden brown on all sides. Remove from the pan and place in a large casserole. Blend the flour and curry powder into the fat remaining in the pan and cook for 2 minutes. Gradually stir in the stock, and bring to the boil, stirring all the time. Add the chutney, lemon juice and seasoning and pour over the meat balls in the casserole. Cover and cook in a moderate oven 180°C (350°F), Gas Mark 4 for 1 hour. Remove from the oven, stir in the cream, then return to the oven for a further 5 minutes, just to heat the cream, but it must not be allowed to boil after the cream has been added. Taste and adjust the seasoning and serve with boiled rice and a tossed green salad. *Serves 12.*

Mixed Fish Pie

A hot fish pie can be a very successful buffet party dish and by adding some of the cheaper shellfish, such as cockles and mussels, and just a few prawns and some squid you can make it interesting, without it becoming too expensive.

*1 squid, weighing about 650 g
  (1½ lb)*
6 dl (1 pint) water
1 onion, peeled and chopped
1 small bay leaf
peeled rind of 1 lemon
*salt and freshly milled black
  pepper*
3 dl (½ pint) dry cider
*900 g (2 lb) white fish, e.g.
  cod, coley, huss*
*225 g (8 oz) butter or mar-
  garine*
225 g (8 oz) flour

1.2 litres (2 pints) milk
*500 g (18 oz) packet frozen
  cockles*
*500 g (18 oz) packet frozen
  mussels*
225 g (8 oz) frozen prawns

For the potato topping:
2.2 kg (5 lb) potatoes
salt
3 dl (½ pint) milk
*100 g (4 oz) butter or mar-
  garine*

Clean the squid, removing the stomach, intestines and ink sacs. Chop the tentacles and cut the body into narrow slices. Put the water into a pan with the onion, the bay leaf, lemon rind and seasoning. Bring to the boil, then lower the heat, add the squid and poach gently for 30 minutes or until tender. Strain, reserving the cooking liquor. Put the cider into a pan, add the white fish, cover the pan and poach gently for 10 minutes or until tender. Remove from the heat, allow to cool in the cooking liquor, then skin and flake the fish and reserve the cooking liquor.

Melt the margarine or butter in a large pan, add the flour and cook for a minute. Gradually stir in the milk, the cider from cooking the white fish, and the liquor from cooking the squid and bring to the boil, stirring all the time. Remove from the heat. Rinse the cockles as suggested on the packet, then add to the sauce together with the mussels, squid, white fish and prawns. Mix well, season to taste, then turn into two large ovenproof dishes.

Peel the potatoes and cook in boiling salted water until tender. Drain well and sieve or mash thoroughly with the milk, butter or margarine and plenty of seasoning. Beat well, then put into a piping bag fitted with a large rose pipe and pipe all over the top of both the dishes so that the fish is completely covered. Bake in a moderately hot oven, 200°C (400°F), Gas Mark 6 for 40 minutes or until the pie is piping hot. Serve with a green and/or tomato salad.   *Serves 20*

Spinach and Lasagne Rolls

I have always found it very difficult to stuff cannelloni as in the process of stuffing the pasta it always seems to break on me and I think it is much easier to spread a filling on lasagne and then roll it up. In some supermarkets and delicatessens you can sometimes buy the end of the ham, which has become difficult to slice, slightly cheaper than normal, and a piece like this would be ideal here.

salt
2 tablespoons oil
450 g (1 lb) lasagne
3 medium-sized onions,
  peeled and chopped
650 g (1½ lb) cooked
  spinach, chopped
350 g (12 oz) cooked ham or
  bacon, diced

freshly milled black pepper
100 g (4 oz) butter or margarine
100 g (4 oz) flour
1.2 litres (2 pints) milk
450 g (1 lb) Cheddar cheese,
  grated.

Bring a large pan of salted water to the boil, add 1 tablespoon of the oil, then the lasagne, piece by piece, and cook for about 8 minutes. Drain and lay out to dry on a clean, damp tea towel. Heat the remaining oil in a pan. Add the onions and fry gently for 5 minutes. Remove from the heat, add the spinach and ham, mix well and season with salt and pepper. Divide the spinach mixture between the pieces of lasagne, spread evenly over the pasta, then roll each one up firmly and place in an ovenproof dish.

Melt the butter or margarine in a pan, add the flour and cook for a minute. Gradually stir in the milk and bring to the boil, stirring all the time. Add three-quarters of the cheese and cook, stirring until the cheese has melted. Remove from the heat and season to taste. Pour over the lasagne rolls and sprinkle with the remaining cheese. Bake in a moderately hot oven, 190°C (375°F), Gas Mark 5 for about 40 minutes or until the top is golden brown. *Serves 10*

Beef Curry

A good curry has a lot to recommend it as a buffet party dish. Firstly the flavour will, if anything, improve if it is made a day or two beforehand, allowed to cool and then reheated. Because of the long, slow cooking you can use the cheapest stewing steak (provided you remove the fat and gristle) and, apart from your big steaming pan of curry, the only other hot dish you need prepare is boiled rice which, especially if you use easy-cook rice, couldn't be simpler. Obviously one of the nicest things about a curry is all the little side dishes of chutney, raw vegetables, fruit, yogurt, etc., which go with it and here you must exercise a little restraint without cutting back completely, or you will find that any money you have saved on your economical curry has all been frittered away on these! Poppadums are fairly inexpensive and you can cook them several hours before they are required, and then just warm them up in the oven. Bowls of natural yogurt with finely chopped cucumber (provided this is not too expensive) and garlic added, finely chopped or sliced onion, desiccated or grated fresh coconut, home-made chutney – all these are fairly inexpensive and no-one will ever notice that expensive mango chutneys, tomatoes in the depths of winter, etc., are missing.

6 tablespoons oil
450 g (1 lb) onions peeled and chopped
8 cloves of garlic, crushed
1.8 kg (4 lb) stewing beef
5 cm (2 inch) piece of fresh root ginger, peeled and finely chopped
2 tablespoons ground coriander
6 cardamoms, crushed

1 tablespoon ground cumin
2 tablespoons garam masala
1 tablespoon chilli powder
2 teaspoons ground fenugreek
salt
6 dl (1 pint) beef stock
900 g (2 lb) potatoes, peeled and diced
3 dl (½ pint) natural yogurt

Heat the oil in a large fireproof casserole and gently fry the onions and garlic for 5 minutes. Cut the beef into 2.5 cm (1 inch) dice, add to the pan together with the ginger, spices and salt and cook gently for 10 minutes, stirring frequently. Gradually stir in the stock and bring to the boil, stirring all the time. Cover the casserole and put into a slow oven, 150°C (300°F), Gas Mark 2 for 2½ hours. Add the potatoes and continue cooking for a further 30 minutes. Stir in the yogurt just before serving. *Serves 12*

Savoury Stuffed Pancakes

You can prepare these pancakes in advance and freeze them together with their filling and sauce; but if you do this you should add 2 tablespoons of oil to the pancake batter which will improve their keeping quality.

6 dl (1 pint) pancake batter
    (page 190)
oil or fat for frying
900 g (2 lb) minced beef
4 large onions, peeled and
    chopped
4 cloves of garlic, crushed
3 sticks celery, chopped
794 g (1 lb 12 oz) can
    tomatoes

1 teaspoon chilli powder
2 teaspoons dried thyme
salt
50 g (2 oz) butter or mar-
    garine
50 g (2 oz) flour
6 dl (1 pint) milk
150 g (6 oz) Cheddar cheese,
    grated
freshly milled black pepper

Make up the pancake batter as in the recipe on page 190 and use to make about 20 pancakes. As you make the pancakes, separate each one with a piece of greaseproof paper and pile on a plate. Fry the beef, without any fat, in a large pan for about 5 minutes, then add the onions, garlic and celery and cook for a further 10 minutes, stirring frequently. Add the tomatoes, chilli powder, thyme and salt. Cover the pan and simmer gently for 45 minutes. Taste and adjust the seasoning. Divide the beef mixture between the pancakes, roll each one up and place in a large ovenproof dish.

Melt the butter or margarine in a pan, add the flour and cook for a minute, then gradually stir in the milk and bring to the boil, stirring all the time. Add the cheese, cook over a gentle heat until it has melted, then taste and adjust the seasoning. Pour over the pancakes and bake in a moderately hot oven, 190°C (375°F), Gas Mark 5 for about 40 minutes or until the top is golden brown *Serves 10*

Smoked Haddock Lasagne

This may sound a rather strange combination, but tastes surprisingly good. You can make it with yellow lasagne, but it looks more attractive with green as this provides a contrast with the yellow fish sauce.

salt
1 tablespoon oil
650 g (1½ lb) lasagne
1.2 litres (2 pints) milk
1 bay leaf
1 onion, peeled and quartered
900 g (2 lb) smoked haddock
75 g (3 oz) butter or margarine
75 g (3 oz) flour
1 green pepper

freshly milled black pepper

For the topping:
6 eggs
6 tablespoons milk
salt and freshly milled black pepper
25 g (1 oz) butter or margarine
100 g (4 oz) Cheddar cheese, grated

Bring a large pan of salted water to the boil. Add the oil (this helps to keep the lasagne separate and prevent it from sticking together) then the lasagne, piece by piece. Cook for about 8 minutes or until the lasagne is nearly tender, then drain and leave to dry on a damp tea towel.

Put the milk, bay leaf and onion into a pan with the haddock. Cover and poach gently for about 10 minutes or until the haddock is quite tender. Remove the haddock from the pan, skin, flake and remove any bones, strain and reserve the milk. Melt the butter or margarine in a pan. Add the flour and cook for a minute, then gradually stir in the reserved milk and bring to the boil, stirring all the time until the sauce thickens. Blanch the pepper in boiling water for 2 minutes, then drain and cut into small pieces, discarding the core and seeds. Add the pepper to the sauce with the fish and season to taste with plenty of freshly milled black pepper and a little salt.

Put a layer of lasagne in the bottom of an ovenproof dish, cover with a layer of sauce and repeat these layers, ending with a layer of lasagne. Beat the eggs with the milk and seasoning. Melt the remaining butter or margarine in a pan and scramble the eggs until they are almost set, then spoon over the top of the lasagne. Sprinkle with the cheese and bake in a moderately hot oven, 190°C (375°F), Gas Mark 5 for 45 minutes. *Serves 12*

Smoked Haddock Mousse

If you prefer you can use smoked cod for this or, if you can get it, smoked whiting which is generally cheaper.

450 g (1 lb) smoked haddock
3 dl (½ pint) water
1 packet aspic or enough aspic crystals to set 3 dl (½ pint)
2 eggs, separated
grated rind and juice of ½ lemon

1 to 2 tablespoons dry sherry (optional)
½ teaspoon anchovy essence
1.5 dl (¼ pint) double cream, lightly whipped

To garnish:
sliced cucumber

Poach the haddock in the water for 10 minutes or until it is just cooked. Remove from the pan, take off the skin and flake the fish finely. Using the liquid from poaching the fish, make the aspic up to 3 dl (½ pint) following the instructions on the packet and using a little extra water if necessary. Beat the egg yolks with the lemon rind and juice, sherry, if using, and anchovy essence. Beat in the cooled aspic, then stir in the flaked fish. Put the mixture on one side and allow to stiffen slightly.

Whisk the egg whites until they are stiff and fold first the cream and then the egg whites into the haddock mixture. Turn into a mould or lightly oiled 17.5 cm (7 inch) cake tin and refrigerate until set. Turn the mousse out and garnish with sliced cucumber before serving. *Serves 8*

Corn and Kipper Salad

Poor man's smoked salmon is how raw kippers are frequently referred to, and they are certainly one of my favourites. Make sure you marinate them for at least 2 hours before serving, as this improves the flavour enormously. I generally buy frozen kipper fillets, as they are very easy to skin when they are still frozen, or partially frozen. If you wished you could use 'kippered' mackerel fillets.

350 g (12 oz) kipper fillets
juice of 1 lemon
1 green pepper, seeded and
  chopped
1 red pepper, seeded and
  chopped
326 g (12 oz) can sweetcorn
  kernels

4 spring onions, chopped
1 teaspoon made mustard
4 tablespoons oil
freshly milled black pepper
salt, if necessary
1 bunch watercress

Skin the kipper fillets and cut diagonally into thin strips, about 0.75 cm (¼ inch) wide and 5 cm (2 inch) long. Put into a basin, pour over the lemon juice and leave to marinate for at least 2 hours. Add all the remaining ingredients, toss the mixture together and season to taste with pepper, and salt if necessary. Turn onto a serving plate, and garnish with the bunch of watercress. *Serves 6 to 8*

Cheese and Courgette Flan

This makes a rather pleasant change from the usual egg and bacon, and cheese and spinach flans.

225 g (8 oz) shortcrust pastry
  (page 187)
2 tablespoons oil
2 medium-sized onions,
  peeled and chopped
650 g (1½ lb) courgettes

4 eggs, beaten
3 dl (½ pint) milk
salt and freshly milled black
  pepper
150 g (6 oz) double Glouces-
  ter cheese, grated

Roll out the pastry and use to line a 27.5 cm (11 inch) flan tin or dish. Prick the base with a fork and fill the centre with a circle of greaseproof paper and some baking beans. Bake in a moderately hot oven, 190°C (375°F), Gas Mark 5 for 15 minutes. Remove the greaseproof paper and beans and bake for a further 5 minutes to dry out the base.

While the pastry is cooking, heat the oil in a pan and gently fry the onions for 5 minutes. Cut the courgettes into thin 0.75 cm (¼ inch) slices, add to the onions, cover the pan and cook very gently for 10 to 15 minutes. Drain the courgettes and onions then put into the base of the flan case. Beat the eggs, then beat in the milk and the liquid drained from the courgettes. Season with salt and plenty of black pepper. Pour this over the courgettes and sprinkle the cheese on top. Return to the oven and bake for 30 minutes or until the filling is set and the top is golden brown. Serve cold, or make in advance and reheat before serving.   *Serves 8*

Prawn and Cucumber Flan

Prawns are one of my favourite foods, but these days I find them so expensive, I have to use them sparingly with other ingredients to cut down the cost.

225 g (8 oz) shortcrust pastry (page 187)	*4 eggs, beaten*
	100 g (4 oz) peeled prawns
225 g (8 oz) white fish fillets	*½ cucumber, peeled and*
4.5 dl (¾ pint) milk	*diced*
salt and freshly milled black pepper	*½ bunch spring onions, finely chopped*

Roll out the pastry and use to line a 27.5 cm (11 inch) flan tin or dish. Prick the base lightly with a fork and fill the centre with a circle of greaseproof paper and some baking beans. Bake in a moderately hot oven 190°C (375°F), Gas Mark 5 for 15 minutes. Remove the paper and beans and bake for a further 5 minutes to dry out the base.

While the pastry is cooking, put the fish into a small pan. Pour over the milk and season with salt and pepper. Cover the pan and poach gently for about 10 minutes or until the fish is tender. Drain the fish thoroughly, then remove the skin and bones and flake. Beat the eggs, strain in the milk from cooking the fish, beat well and season with salt and pepper. Place the prawns (any liquid from frozen prawns can be added to the beaten eggs), cooked fish, cucumber, and spring onions in the base of the cooked flan. Pour over the egg and milk and bake for about 30 minutes or until the filling is set. Serve cold. *Serves 8*

Chicken Paprika

Make this dish with a large (or 2 small) boiling chickens, which you can usually buy quite cheaply, either fresh or frozen. The length of time a boiling chicken takes to cook can vary between 2 and 4 hours, but as you have to cook this the day before you want to serve it, you won't have the embarrassment of guests sitting twiddling their thumbs or drinking you out of house and home waiting for it to be tender! I have also served it hot very successfully, or you can make it into curried chicken by replacing the paprika with curry powder.

2.7 kg (6 lb) boiling chicken
  or 2 smaller ones
1 onion, peeled
1 blade of mace
6 peppercorns
a sprig of thyme
a few sprigs of parsley
peeled rind of 1 lemon
1 teaspoon salt
1 litre (scant 2 pints) water

For the sauce:
50 g (2 oz) butter
40 g (1½ oz) flour
1 tablespoon paprika
7.5 dl (1¼ pints) chicken
  stock (from cooking the
  chicken)
2 tablespoons redcurrant jelly
1.5 dl (¼ pint) soured cream
  or yogurt
salt and freshly milled black
  pepper

Put the chicken into a saucepan with the onion, mace, peppercorns, thyme, parsley, lemon rind, salt and water. Cover and bring to the boil. Simmer for 2 to 4 hours, depending on the chicken, until it is very tender. Remove from the heat and allow to cool in the cooking liquor.

Skim off any fat from the top of the cooking liquor, strain and reserve 7.5 dl (1¼ pints) for the sauce. Remove the chicken from the bones, discard the skin and cut into bite-size pieces.

Melt the butter for the sauce in a pan. Stir in the flour and paprika and cook for 2 minutes without browning. Gradually stir in the reserved chicken stock and bring to the boil, stirring all the time. Simmer gently for 5 minutes. Remove from the heat and stir in the redcurrant jelly until it has dissolved. Cover the sauce with a circle of damp greaseproof paper and allow to cool. When the sauce is quite cold, remove the greaseproof paper and stir in the cream or yogurt and seasoning to taste. Add the chicken pieces and stir until they are evenly coated with the sauce. Turn onto a serving dish and garnish with a sprinkling of extra paprika and some parsley or watercress, or a circle of rice salad.   *Serves 10*

French Pork Terrine

If you do not have a suitable terrine you can cook this in a loaf tin, or even a roasting tin. I usually serve it ready-sliced, so that the greedy can't cut themselves too large a hunk!

8 rashers streaky bacon
450 g (1 lb) pork fillet or use a piece of lean pork from the leg
25 g (1 oz) butter
1 medium-sized onion, peeled and finely chopped
100 g (4 oz) mushrooms, finely chopped
225 g (8 oz) pig's liver

225 g (8 oz) fat pork
50 g (2 oz) fresh white bread-crumbs
1 tablespoon brandy (optional)
2 teaspoons freshly chopped thyme
1 tablespoon chopped parsley
salt and freshly milled black pepper

Cut off the rind from the bacon rashers. Place the rashers on a board and stretch them with the back of a knife. Use six of them to line the base and sides of a terrine or loaf tin. Slit the pork fillets, or, if using, cut leg of pork into slices. Place the meat between two sheets of greaseproof paper and beat with a mallet or rolling pin to flatten them. Melt the butter in a pan and gently fry the onion for 5 minutes. Add the mushrooms and cook for a further 5 minutes. Mince the liver and fat pork and add to the onion and mushrooms with the remaining ingredients. Mix well. Put a third of the minced mixture into the prepared terrine or tin and cover with half the pork fillet, then a layer of minced mixture, the remaining pork fillet, and finally the last of the minced mixture. Lay the remaining bacon rashers on top. Cover tightly with foil and a lid. Stand the terrine or tin in a roasting pan containing 2.5 cm (1 inch) of cold water and bake in a very moderate oven, 170°C (325°F), Gas Mark 3 for 2½ hours. Remove from the oven and stand a weight on top of the foil to press the terrine while it is cooling.   *Serves 10 to 12*

Spanish Pâté

This pâté has stuffed olives packed into it, so that it looks most attractive when sliced.

6 rashers streaky bacon
100 g (4 oz) chicken livers
225 g (8 oz) pig's liver
250 g (10 oz) boned pork
  belly
150 g (6 oz) fat bacon
100 g (4 oz) minced beef

salt and freshly milled black
  pepper
¼ teaspoon ground mace
1 teaspoon dried mixed herbs
4 tablespoons sherry
2 cloves of garlic, crushed
50 g (2 oz) stuffed green
  olives

Cut off the rind from the bacon. Place the bacon on a board and stretch with the back of a knife. Use to line a 650 g (1½ lb) loaf tin. Mince the chicken livers, pig's liver, pork belly and fat bacon. Put into a bowl and add the beef, salt and pepper, mace, herbs, sherry and garlic. Mix well. Turn the pâté into the prepared loaf tin, but arrange the olives in it at various levels in various places. Cover with foil and stand in a roasting tin containing 2.5 cm (1 inch) of cold water. Bake in a slow oven, 150°C (300°F), Gas Mark 2 for 2 hours. Remove from the oven and stand a weight on top of the pâté to press it while it is cooling. Turn out and cut into slices before serving. *Serves 10*

Ballotine de Canard or Boned and Stuffed Duck

Whenever I serve this, it is what the French would describe as a *succès fou* – it looks very impressive, tastes out of this world and is nothing like as complicated to make as most people imagine. True it does take a bit of time to bone the duck, especially on one's first attempt, but I think you will find the end result well worth the effort.

1 duck, weighing about 2.2 kg (5 lb)
salt and freshly milled black pepper
3 oranges
25 g (1 oz) butter
350 g (12 oz) lean pork
350 g (12 oz) lean veal
2 tablespoons brandy (optional)

2 teaspoons freshly chopped marjoram
1 teaspoon freshly chopped rosemary

To garnish:
1 to 2 oranges, sliced
watercress

First of all make sure you have a good, small to medium-sized, sharp knife. Put the duck, breast-side down, on a wooden board. With the knife cut through the back skin and flesh to the backbone, then carefully work the flesh away from the carcass, pressing the knife closely against the carcass and taking all the meat away from the bone with the skin. Remove the bones from the legs and wings by scraping the flesh away from the bones, but try not to split the skin. Leave the drum-stick bones in place. When all the other bones have been removed, lay the duck out flat and remove any excess fat, then sprinkle with salt and pepper. Peel the oranges, so that all the white pith is removed, then cut them in half lengthways.

Melt the butter in a small pan and fry the duck liver for about 4 minutes. Remove from the pan and mince with the pork and veal. Put the minced mixture into a bowl, add the brandy, if using, and the herbs and seasoning. The seasoning is important and to check that I have added sufficient, I usually put about a teaspoonful of the mixture into a non-stick frying pan, fry it until it is cooked and then taste it and adjust the seasoning accordingly.

Spread half the pork and veal mixture on to the duck, then lay the orange halves along the centre of the duck, with their cut sides uppermost. Spread the remaining pork and veal mixture on top. Fold in the ends of the duck, then bring the sides into the centre to form a parcel. Sew with fine string or coarse thread, and if you have made any holes in the duck skin, sew these at the same time. Turn the duck breast-side up and place in a roasting tin. Season the outside with salt and pepper and roast in a moderate oven, 180°C (350°F), Gas Mark 4, for about 1½ hours. Remove from the oven and allow to cool. To serve the duck, cut into slices, starting from the front end, but leave the drumstick bones still intact and garnish with orange slices and watercress. *Serves 10*

Lentil Salad

This is a good winter salad, but you must use green or brown lentils, and not the bright orange ones, as these break up and become mushy almost as soon as they are cooked. Green or brown lentils are not difficult to find, either in health food stores or in Asian or Continental grocers.

450 g (1 lb) lentils
1.8 litres (3 pints) stock
1.5 dl (¼ pint) French dressing
2 medium-sized onions, peeled and very finely chopped

2 tablespoons chopped parsley

To garnish:
tomato slices or wedges or 1 onion, peeled and cut into rings

Pick over the lentils, then put into a pan with the stock. Cover the pan, bring to the boil and cook gently for about 1 hour or until the lentils are tender, but not mushy. Strain well, turn into a bowl and while still hot, pour over the French dressing. Add the onions and parsley and toss together. Leave until quite cold, then turn into a serving bowl; provided they are not too expensive the salad looks very attractive garnished with a few slices or wedges of tomato, otherwise I use a few onion rings. *Serves 12*

Corn and Potato Salad

I find that potato salad made entirely with mayonnaise can be rather heavy and cloying; using half mayonnaise and half soured cream makes a lighter dressing with a very pleasant flavour.

1.8 kg (4 lb) potatoes
salt
3 dl (½ pint) mayonnaise
3 dl (½ pint) soured cream
freshly milled black pepper

326 g (12 oz) can sweetcorn kernels
4 sticks celery, finely chopped
4 tablespoons chopped chives
a little milk (see method)

Scrub the potatoes and cook in boiling salted water until just tender. Drain well, peel when cool enough to handle and cut into 1.5 cm (½ inch) dice. Put into a large bowl, add the mayonnaise and soured cream, mix well, season and leave until the potatoes are quite cold. Drain the sweetcorn, and add to the potatoes with the celery and most of the chives.

Taste and adjust the seasoning and if the mixture is a little too thick, add some milk to soften it. Turn into a serving dish and sprinkle with the remaining chives before serving.   *Serves 12*

Red Bean Salad

This salad looks very pretty, as the beans contrast well with the pale yellow of the mayonnaise.

450 g (1 lb) red kidney beans
1 bouquet garni
salt
3 dl (½ pint) mayonnaise

2 tablespoons chopped parsley
1 bunch spring onions, finely chopped

Soak the beans overnight in cold water, drain well, put into a saucepan and cover with fresh cold water. Add the bouquet garni and season with salt. Cover the pan, bring to the boil, then simmer gently for 2½ hours or until the beans are quite tender. Drain well, and while still hot, stir in the mayonnaise, parsley, spring onions and seasoning. Season to taste and allow to cool.   *Serves 12*

Courgette and Tomato Salad

Courgettes are usually one of the cheapest vegetables in late summer and early autumn, and, as they are easy to grow and so prolific, even people like me, with only a cabbage patch, cultivate them.

900 g (2 lb) courgettes
5 tablespoons oil
3 tablespoons lemon juice
3 dl (½ pint) water
1 bay leaf
1 sprig thyme

1 sprig marjoram (optional)
10 coriander seeds, crushed
salt and freshly milled black pepper
450 g (1 lb) tomatoes, peeled and chopped

Wipe the courgettes and cut them into diagonal slices about 1.5 cm (½ inch) thick. Put the oil, lemon juice, water, bay

leaf, thyme, marjoram, if using, coriander seeds and seasoning into a pan and bring to the boil. Add the courgettes and
tomatoes and cook, uncovered, over a moderate heat for
about 30 minutes. Remove from the heat, allow to cool and
discard the herbs. Chill lightly before serving. *Serves 8 to 10*

Red Cabbage, Apple and Yogurt Salad

Red cabbage makes a pleasant change from green in a slaw,
although you could of course use ordinary hard white cabbage
if you preferred.

650 g (1½ lb) red cabbage
2 green dessert apples, cored
  and chopped
1 tablespoon lemon juice
4 sticks celery, finely chopped

1 medium-sized onion, peeled
  and very finely chopped
3 dl (½ pint) natural yogurt
salt and freshly milled black
  pepper

Discard any very tough outer leaves of the cabbage and shred
the remainder finely, discarding the central core. Toss the
apples in the lemon juice to preserve the colour then put into
a large bowl with the cabbage, celery and onion. Add the
yogurt, mix well and season to taste with salt and pepper.
Turn into a serving bowl and leave for at least 1 hour before
serving for the flavours to infuse. *Serves 10*

Rice Salad

This is a basic recipe for rice salad, which you can vary according to what you have in your store cupboard, the time of the
year and what is in season. I personally think a rice salad is
improved by the addition of something sweet, such as the
dried apricots I have suggested, but you could use raisins,
oranges, etc., if you preferred. So that the rice really does
have a good flavour it is most important to add the French
dressing to it while it is still warm so that the dressing can soak
into it as it cools.

450 g (1 lb) long grain rice
salt
1 bunch spring onions, chopped
1 large green or red pepper, seeded and chopped

100 g (4 oz) dried apricots, finely chopped
1.5 dl (¼ pint) French dressing
½ cucumber, finely diced

Cook the rice in boiling salted water until tender. While the rice is cooking put the spring onions, pepper and apricots into a large bowl. Drain the rice well, add to the ingredients in the bowl and toss lightly together. Pour in the dressing and toss very well, so that the rice is thoroughly coated with the dressing. Allow to cool, and stir in the cucumber shortly before serving. *Serves 12*

Pasta Salad

I make a number of salads with pasta, using the different shapes available, or I just use spaghetti and break it into short pieces. You can dress them either with mayonnaise, as in this recipe, or a French dressing, soured cream or yogurt. Add any other ingredients you like, such as red and green peppers, corn, cooked beans, tomatoes, etc. For simple family meals, pasta salads make a very good, economical main course as you can eke out a small amount of cooked meat, fish or poultry by adding it to cooked pasta, together with a dressing and some chopped, cooked or raw vegetables and serving it with a green and/or tomato salad.

225 g (8 oz) pasta
salt
1.5 dl (¼ pint) mayonnaise
225 g (8 oz) cooked peas
1 bunch spring onions, finely chopped

1 small head fennel, finely chopped
freshly milled black pepper

To garnish:
3 tomatoes, quartered

Cook the pasta in boiling salted water until just tender. Drain and rinse under running cold water until quite cool. Dry thoroughly, then mix with the remaining ingredients and season well with salt and pepper. Turn into a serving bowl and garnish with the tomatoes before serving.   *Serves 10*

Bean Sprout Salad

Bean sprouts can be found in many greengrocers and supermarkets these days, and I find them particularly good value in the winter when other green salad vegetables are very expensive. They do not store very well, so you should keep them in the vegetable compartment in the fridge and use them at least the day after you have bought them. If you have difficulty in buying them or are sufficiently enthusiastic about it, you can grow your own very simply by spreading some mung beans on wet blotting paper, in the way one grew mustard and cress at school, and they grow in about 4 days.

450 g (1 lb) bean sprouts
2 medium-sized oranges
½ cucumber

1 bunch watercress
1.5 dl (¼ pint) French dressing

Pick over the bean sprouts, wash them in cold water and dry well. Peel the oranges, discarding all the white pith, and cut into segments, discarding all the skin, membrane and pith. Dice the cucumber, trim off the stalks from the watercress, wash and dry well. Place all the vegetables and the orange segments in a salad bowl, pour over the dressing and toss lightly.   *Serves 12*

Green Salad

A green salad is almost an essential dish, certainly for cold buffets, and very often for hot buffets as well, as it is much easier to prepare than cooked vegetables for a large number of people. In summer this does not generally present too many problems, but in winter green salad vegetables tend to be expensive, so one wants to look around and see what else one can use, other than the usual round lettuces.

There are several varieties of winter lettuce, such as endive and batavia, and these are surprisingly bulky once they have been broken down into small pieces. Chinese cabbages, or Chinese leaves as they are also known, are widely available, and these can also provide a good substitute for lettuce. Whilst a hard white or Dutch cabbage is used for coleslaw, the cheaper cabbage also makes a good base for a salad, as do brussels sprouts. Choose the large, bushier sprouts for salad, remove the very outside leaves, wash them thoroughly and then shred.

Both winter and summer I like to give variety to the salad, by adding watercress, mustard and cress, very thinly sliced green pepper, chopped chicory, thin strips of Florence fennel, finely chopped celery, and anything else which looks fresh, is in season and cheap when I go to the greengrocers. I think green salads are vastly improved by the addition of some chopped herbs, and whilst this is more difficult in winter, there is always parsley, and often chives, as well. In summer you can also add chopped chervil, a very little chopped mint, lemon balm, fennel, basil, etc.

If you are expecting people to eat the salad standing up with a fork, make sure that you tear the lettuce leaves etc into pieces which are easy to pick up and eat this way. Also make sure that the salad is really crisp. Wash it in cold water and dry well, first either in a colander or salad shaker, and then pat dry in a clean tea towel. Put it into a polythene bag in the fridge for at least an hour to crisp up, then put into the salad bowl. Do not pour the dressing over the salad and toss it until just before serving, and make sure you toss it so that every leaf is coated with dressing, but that it is not swimming in it.

Raw Carrot Salad

Grated raw carrot can provide one of the cheapest salads, especially for winter parties. I simply peel, then grate the carrots and toss in a French dressing, made with lemon juice rather than vinegar, with a little chopped parsley, or perhaps a few black olives. Turnips, especially young turnips, are also very good served this way, and you can either mix them with the carrot or serve them on their own. Grated raw celeriac also combines well with grated carrot, but you must toss it in the dressing as soon as you have grated it or it will lose its colour.

Beetroot Salad

Never add beetroot to other salads or the entire salad will become pink. For some reason in England beetroot is almost always cut into slices, but these are far too big for buffet parties, so I always dice mine and toss it in a French dressing with a little very finely chopped onion, spring onions or chives and usually add some finely chopped capers as well. Yogurt also makes a good dressing for beetroot instead of a French dressing.

Cucumber Salad

Cucumbers are generally far too expensive to be included in winter salads, but are excellent for the summer. I prefer to peel the cucumber, but this is obviously a matter of choice, and in fact the cucumber is more digestible if the skin is left on. Owing to the high percentage of water in a cucumber it is best if you salt it before serving. Cut the cucumber into thin slices, put into a colander and sprinkle with a teaspoon of salt. Leave for about 30 minutes for the excess liquid to drain off, then pat it dry with kitchen paper. Toss in French dressing, or cucumber is of course excellent mixed with yogurt and chopped fresh mint.

Coleslaw

Coleslaw is the most popular winter salad. For a basic cole-slaw, finely shred 450 g (1 lb cabbage) add a grated onion,

100 g (4 oz) grated carrot and 1.5 dl (¼ pint) mayonnaise. Mix well and season to taste with salt and pepper. You can then add any ingredients you like, such as sultanas or raisins, chopped walnuts or hazelnuts, chopped pineapple or apples, tossed in lemon juice to prevent them from browning, etc.

Apricot Cheesecake

This is an easy dessert to make which freezes well. If you want to freeze it, instead of using a 794 g (1 lb 12 oz) can of apricots, use a 400 g (14 oz) can for the cheesecake, then when you want to serve it, use the contents of a second 400 g (14 oz can) to decorate it. I have suggested making it with canned apricots, but it is even better if made with fresh apricots when these are in season and cheap.

For the filling:
1 packet orange jelly
794 g (l lb 12 oz) can apricots
450 g (1 lb) cottage cheese,
   sieved
2 tablespoons sugar
1.5 dl (¼ pint) double cream,
   lightly whipped

2 tablespoons soft brown
   sugar
150 g (6 oz) ginger biscuits,
   crushed

To glaze:
2 tablespoons apricot jam
2 teaspoons water

For the crust:
75 g (3 oz) butter or margarine

Put the jelly into a pan with 3 tablespoons of juice from the can of apricots. Put over a very gentle heat and stir from time to time until the jelly has dissolved; it must not be allowed to boil. Reserve 6 apricot halves for decoration, drain and finely chop, sieve or blend the remainder. Stir in the cottage cheese with the sugar. Stir in the jelly, then carefully fold in the whipped cream. Turn into a 20 to 22.5 cm (8 to 9 inch) loose-bottomed cake tin or springform pan. Chill until set.

Melt the butter or margarine in a pan, add the sugar and crumbs and mix well. Sprinkle over the top of the cheesecake, then press down lightly. Chill for a further 1 hour.

Turn the cheesecake out, by inverting on to a serving plate. Decorate with the remaining apricots. Sieve the apricot jam into a pan, stir in the water and bring to the boil. Remove from the heat and allow to cool, then brush over the apricots and the top of the cheesecake to make a glaze.

Serves 8 to 10

Crunchy Chocolate Mousse

I love crisply fried brown breadcrumbs and these give a very pleasant contrast in texture as a topping for a chocolate mousse. If you wanted you could add a couple of tablespoons of rum or brandy to the chocolate mousse (add this to the custard before you add the egg whites), or if you are feeling really extravagant, you can spread the top of the mousse with a layer of whipped cream before sprinkling over the breadcrumbs.

15 g (½ oz) powdered
  gelatine
4 tablespoons water
4.5 dl (¾ pint) milk
3 eggs, separated
25 g (1 oz) caster sugar
½ teaspoon vanilla essence

413 g (4 oz) packet chocolate
  chips
25 g (1 oz) butter
50 g (2 oz) fresh brown
  breadcrumbs
25 g (1 oz) soft brown sugar

Sprinkle the gelatine over the water in a small cup and leave to soften. Pour the milk into a pan and bring up to blood heat. Beat the egg yolks with the sugar and vanilla essence in a basin or the top of a double saucepan. Pour over the milk, then stand over a pan of gently simmering water and cook until the custard has thickened, stirring all the time. Stir in the softened gelatine and when this has dissolved, add the choco-late chips and stir until all the chocolate has melted. Remove from the heat and put on one side until the mixture begins to thicken, stirring from time to time. Whisk the egg whites until they form stiff peaks, then fold into the chocolate mixture. Turn into a shallow serving dish and chill for at least 1 hour or until set. Melt the butter in a frying pan and fry the crumbs until they are crisp and golden. Remove from the heat and stir in the sugar. Sprinkle the crumbs over the mousse shortly before serving. *Serves 8*

Blackberry Mousse

Blackberries really are one of the few 'free' foods which are readily available to anyone living within a few miles of the countryside.

900 g (2 lb) blackberries	*1.5 dl (¼ pint) water*
100 g (4 oz) granulated sugar	*6 eggs, separated*
20 g (¾ oz) powdered gelatine	*100 g (4 oz) caster sugar*

Pick over the blackberries and wash them thoroughly in cold water. Drain in a colander, then put into a pan with the granu-lated sugar. Cover and simmer for about 10 minutes. Sprinkle the gelatine over the water in a cup and leave to soften. When the blackberries are soft, add the softened gelatine and stir until it has dissolved. Either sieve the blackberry mixture or put into a blender until smooth and then sieve to remove all the pips. Whisk the egg yolks and caster sugar over a pan of hot water until the mixture is thick and creamy, then remove from the heat and beat in the blackberry purée. Whisk the egg whites until they form stiff peaks, then fold quickly into the blackberry mixture. Turn into a serving dish and chill for at least 2 hours before serving. Serve with single cream.

   Serves 12

Caroline's Plum Flan

This is not the cheapest pudding I have ever made, but it is certainly one of the most delicious and will be particularly popular with people who do not like very sweet desserts.

150 g (6 oz) shortcrust pastry (page 187)
2 tablespoons jam, preferably plum jam
450 g (1 lb) plums
25 to 50 g (1 to 2 oz) soft brown sugar
1.5 dl (¼ pint) double cream
1.5 dl (¼ pint) single cream
50 g (2 oz) plain chocolate

Roll out the pastry and use to line the base of a 25 cm (10 inch) flan tin. Prick the base lightly with a fork and then spread with the jam; this helps to seal the pastry and prevent the plum juice soaking into it. Cut the plums in half, remove the stones and arrange on top of the pastry. Sprinkle with the sugar, the amount will depend on the tartness of the plums. Bake in a moderately hot oven, 190°C (375°F), Gas Mark 5 for about 30 minutes or until the plums are tender and the pastry is golden brown. Remove from the oven and allow to cool.

Pour the double and single cream into a basin and whip until it is thick. Spread over the top of the cool plums. Coarsely grate the chocolate and scatter this over the top of the cream. *Serves 8*

Meringue Cake

I find this a very practical pudding for a buffet party as not only can you prepare it several days in advance, and just wrap it in foil so that the moisture cannot get to it, but as I always make my own mayonnaise for salads, I have some surplus egg whites. You could make the mayonnaise at the same time as you make the meringue, as it keeps well in the fridge, in a covered container. You can vary the fruit according to the time of year: raspberries and strawberries are delicious when they are in season and I often use frozen raspberries as well, but you can also use oranges, red-skinned apples, cored and sliced and dipped in lemon juice to preserve the colour, apricots, bananas, etc. In the winter I frequently use a can of chestnut purée, blend this with the cream and sprinkle it with grated chocolate, which does not work out too expensive.

5 egg whites	*1.5 dl (¼ pint) single cream*
250 g (10 oz) caster sugar	*about 450 g (1 lb) fresh pre-*
1.5 dl (¼ pint) double cream	*pared fruit*

Mark out a large circle, about 30 cm (12 inches) in diameter on a piece of lightly oiled greaseproof paper or on a piece of non-stick silicone paper. Whisk the egg whites until they form stiff peaks then gradually whisk in half the sugar a teaspoon at a time. If whisking by hand, fold in the remainder, but if whisking with a machine, continue to whisk in the sugar gradually. Spread about half the meringue over the marked-out circle, then put the remainder into a piping bag fitted with a large rose pipe. Pipe large swirls round the edge of the circle to make a flan case. Bake in a very cool oven, 110°C (225°F), Gas Mark ¼ for about 6 to 8 hours, or leave overnight, until the meringue is crisp. Remove from the oven and allow to cool, then wrap in foil until required. Whip the double and single cream together until they form soft peaks. Spread over the base of the inside of the meringue cake and pile the fruit on top. *Serves 8 to 10*

Damson and Apple Snow

Although apple snow is one of the first desserts one ever learns to make in any cookery class, because it is *so* easy, I still think it is quite delicious. Combined here with damsons, it has a pleasant sharp taste, without the damsons becoming too overpowering.

450 g (1 lb) cooking apples | 3 teaspoons powdered
450 g (1 lb) damsons | gelatine
150 g (6 oz) sugar (approximately) | 3 eggs, separated
1.5 dl (¼ pint) water | 1 tablespoon chopped nuts

Peel, core and slice the apples and wash the damsons. Put into a pan with the sugar and water, cover and simmer gently for about 15 minutes or until all the fruit is soft. While the fruit is cooking, sprinkle the gelatine over 2 tablespoons water in a basin and leave to soften for 5 minutes. Remove the fruit from the heat, stir in the gelatine and continue stirring until the gelatine has dissolved, then sieve the fruit, and beat in the egg yolks. Taste and add a little extra sugar if necessary. Leave the fruit purée until it is cold, but not set. Whisk the egg whites until they form stiff peaks, then fold into the mixture. Turn into a serving bowl and chill for about 2 hours until set. Sprinkle with the nuts before serving.   *Serves 8 to 10*

Elizabethan Flan

This is in fact a mixture between an old English recipe for an orange tart and the citrus tarts which are particularly popular in the Loire Valley of France.

6 thin-skinned oranges | 150 g (6 oz) butter or margarine
3 tablespoons clear honey |
1.5 dl (¼ pint) water | 225 g (8 oz) caster sugar
225 g (8 oz) shortcrust pastry (page 187) | 75 g (3 oz) flour
 | 1.5 dl (¼ pint) single cream

Wash the oranges, cut into thin slices and put into a dish. Mix the honey with the water, pour over the oranges and leave to soak for 8 hours or overnight. Roll out the pastry and use to line a shallow 30 cm (12 inch) flan tin or dish. Prick the base well and chill for about 15 minutes. Cream the butter or margarine with 150 g (6 oz) sugar until light and fluffy, then beat in the flour and the cream alternately. Spread this mixture evenly over the base of the flan and bake in a moderately hot oven, 190°C (375°F), Gas Mark 5 for about 30 minutes. Remove from the oven and allow to cool.

Turn the oranges, together with the syrup in which they have been soaking, into a pan and simmer gently for about 30 minutes. Drain, reserving the syrup, and cool the orange slices, then arrange attractively over the top of the flan. Add the remaining sugar to the syrup and put the mixture into a small pan over a gentle heat, stirring until the sugar has dissolved. Bring to the boil then boil rapidly until the mixture is reduced to a thick syrup, remove from the heat and spoon carefully over the oranges. *Serves 10*

Drinks Parties

Little nibbles for drinks parties can, almost without one realizing it, end up costing a great deal more than one had bargained for, but as it is generally essential to serve some form of 'eats', I have devised some recipes which are as economical as possible, without being too mundane.

Dips always go down well, so I have given three different recipes, an Avocado Dip, Quick Cheese Dip and a Devilled Ham Dip which uses curd cheese as a base. When you are trying to save money it is worth using curd cheese, which is made from milk, rather than cream cheese which is made from cream and is therefore richer, and more expensive. Always make sure that dips are the correct consistency when you serve them; they should not be too solid, especially if you are serving them with potato crisps or the crisps will break, and equally do not make them too runny or people will have terrible difficulty eating them, and not only will they end up with dip all down their fronts, but after everyone has left the sight of your carpet may be rather distressing!

To serve with dips, you can either opt simply for crisps, or biscuits, or make up some crudités – carrots, cucumber, celery and turnip sticks, pieces of crisp green pepper, radishes, etc., all look attractive and I generally prefer the texture of vegetables to crisps or biscuits. You can prepare the vegetables earlier in the day, put them into a large bowl of iced water and leave to soak, then drain and dry thoroughly before arranging on a platter round the bowl of dip.

Some inexpensive toppings for crisp biscuits for canapés are Sardine Spread, Sausage Pâté and Green Cheese. The garnishing of these little canapés is all-important as this is what makes them appealing. In summer it is fairly easy as there are plenty of cheap fresh tomatoes, radishes, watercress, red peppers, etc., but in winter it is more difficult. Paprika looks attractive sprinkled over the Green Cheese Biscuits and could also be used for the Sausage Pâté, or you can simply strew them with a little cress, or use little pieces of raw carrot, gherkin or stuffed olives.

Hot snacks generally require a bit more preparation, but the Onion and Anchovy Tartlets and the Samosas can be prepared in advance and reheated. American Sausagemeat Balls, which are cooked in the oven, can be prepared in advance, and the Celery and Bacon can also be prepared and only takes a few minutes to grill before serving. The Pignatelles unfortunately really do need to be cooked at the last minute, so this recipe is really only suitable for people who have a responsible teenager (or friend) who doesn't mind standing in the kitchen and frying them for 10 minutes. Once they have been cooked they can be kept warm on a plate in a *very* low oven for about half an hour, and the mixture can be prepared an hour before you wish to fry them.

Sausage Pâté

I was served this at a press party at the Carlton Tower Hotel in London given by the British Sausage Bureau and everyone who was there thought it very good.

225 g (8 oz) pork sausages
1.5 dl (¼ pint) dry cider
1 bay leaf
50 g (2 oz) butter or margarine
1 small onion, peeled and chopped

1 clove of garlic, crushed
salt and freshly milled black pepper
about 25 biscuits, or pieces of toast about 5 cm (2 inches) square

Put the sausages into a pan with the cider and bay leaf. Bring to the boil, cover and simmer gently for 30 minutes. Remove from the heat and allow to cool. Skin the sausages and put into a blender with the butter or margarine, onion, garlic and seasoning. Blend until smooth, adding sufficient cider liquid to give a pasty consistency. Pack into a small container, and put into the fridge for at least 4 hours. To serve, put spoonfuls on to about 25 biscuits and garnish.   *Makes about 25*

Green Cheese Biscuits

If you chop the herbs *very finely indeed* for this, you can pipe it on to the biscuits with a large rose nozzle, otherwise you can pipe it using a plain nozzle or simply pile on to the biscuits using a teaspoon.

225 g (8 oz) curd cheese
2 tablespoons milk
2 tablespoons chopped chives
2 tablespoons chopped parsley

1 small clove of garlic, crushed
salt and freshly milled black pepper
about 30 small biscuits
paprika pepper

Beat the cheese, then beat in the milk, chives, parsley and garlic and season to taste. Pipe or spoon on to the biscuits and sprinkle with the paprika. As this is a fairly firm mixture, you can prepare it some time in advance without the biscuits becoming soft. *Makes about 30*

Sardine Spread

You can also serve this spread like a pâté as a starter for lunch or supper.

124 g (4⅜ oz) can sardines
1 tablespoon lemon juice
100 g (4 oz) curd cheese
1 teaspoon very finely chopped capers
1 gherkin, very finely chopped

a few drops of Tabasco
salt
about 50 small biscuits or pieces of toast about 5 cm (2 inches) square

Empty the can of sardines into a basin and mash, together with the oil from the can. Add the lemon juice and cheese and beat well, then add the capers and gherkins and season with a few drops of Tabasco and salt. Spread on the biscuits or toast and garnish before serving. *Makes about 50*

Kipper Canapés

These kipper canapés taste superb, but as it is difficult to cut the kippers into thin slices, à la smoked salmon, they do not look very elegant, so I just put them on a large platter and strew them with mustard and cress, so that they can't be seen too clearly!

225 g (8 oz) frozen kipper fillets
2 tablespoons lemon juice

10 thin slices brown bread and butter
freshly milled black pepper
⅔ box mustard and cress

While the kippers are still frozen, cut into thin slices parallel with the skin, using a sharp knife. Place the slices in a shallow dish, pour over the lemon juice and leave to marinate for 1 to 2 hours. Remove from the lemon juice and dry on kitchen paper. Place the slices of kipper on the bread and season well with freshly milled black pepper. Cut the crusts off the bread, then cut each slice into four. Place on a serving platter and strew the mustard and cress over the top.   *Makes 40*

Onion and Anchovy Tartlets

I make these in ordinary patty tins which I use for jam tarts, mince pies, etc., which is a good size for a cocktail snack. You can make them in advance and just reheat before serving.

50 g (1¾ oz) can anchovies
25 g (1 oz) butter
650 g (1½ lb) onions, peeled and chopped
3 eggs
3 dl (½ pint) milk

salt and freshly milled black pepper
a good pinch of grated nutmeg
350 g (12 oz) shortcrust pastry (page 187)

Open the can of anchovies and pour the oil into a pan. Add the butter and heat gently until the butter has melted. Add the onions and cook gently, uncovered, for about 30 minutes or until they are very soft and golden. Remove from the heat and allow to cool. Chop the anchovies finely. Beat the eggs, beat in the milk, then add the anchovies and cooked onions, together with all the juices from the pan. Season with salt, pepper and nutmeg.

Roll out the pastry, cut out circles with a 7.5 cm (3 inch) cutter and use to line 30 patty tins. Prick the bases lightly, then divide the filling between them. Bake in a moderately hot oven, 190°C (375°F), Gas Mark 5 for about 20 minutes or until the filling is set and pale golden brown.   *Makes 30*

American Sausagemeat Balls

The Americans excel themselves at making delicious little bits and pieces for cocktail parties. These little sausage balls just use ordinary sausagemeat, but it is flavoured with very finely chopped root ginger. They can be served on their own or with any of the sauces given on pages 115–17.

450 g (1 lb) sausagemeat
1 or 2 cloves garlic, crushed
1 teaspoon ground coriander

2.5 cm (1 inch) piece of root
  ginger, peeled and very
  finely chopped
1 egg, beaten

Put the sausagemeat into a bowl and add the garlic, coriander, ginger and egg. Mix well, then with lightly floured hands, form into small balls, about the size of a walnut. Place on a baking tray, cover and chill until ready to bake. Put into a moderately hot oven 190°C (375°F), Gas Mark 5 for 15 to 20 minutes, remove from the oven, skewer each ball with a cocktail stick and place on a serving platter.   *Makes 20*

Pignatelles

So called because very often when they puff up these potato balls look like fir cones. They are similar to a cheese aigrette, but not quite as rich and the addition of potato makes them much cheaper.

450 g (1 lb) potatoes
salt
65 g (2½ oz) plain flour
50 g (2 oz) margarine
1.5 dl (¼ pint) water
3 eggs

150 g (6 oz) strong Cheddar
  cheese, grated
50 g (2 oz) garlic sausage,
  very finely chopped
freshly milled black pepper
deep oil or fat for frying

Scrub the potatoes, but do not peel them. Cook in boiling salted water until tender, then drain and when cool enough to handle, peel and sieve. Sift the flour and a pinch of salt on to a piece of greaseproof paper. Put the margarine and water into a pan and heat gently until the margarine has melted, then bring to the boil. Add the flour all at once, while the pan is still on a low heat. Beat well until the mixture forms a soft ball that leaves the sides of the pan clean. Remove from the heat and allow to cool slightly, then beat in the eggs, one at a time. When the pastry is thick and smooth, beat in the potato purée, then the cheese and garlic sausage. Season to taste. Heat the oil or fat and when hot drop in teaspoonfuls of the mixture. Cook until they are golden brown and puffed up, remove with a draining spoon and dry on kitchen paper. Serve as soon as possible after cooking. *Makes 50*

Samosas

Most readers will be familiar with samosas – those triangular little deep-fried puffs which they sell in Indian grocers and take-aways. They make very good cocktail snacks, provided they are not too spicy, and they have the great advantage that they can be made in advance and reheated in the oven.

150 g (6 oz) plain flour
salt
50 g (2 oz) soft margarine
1.2 dl (4 fl oz) natural yogurt
   or curds from sour milk

For the filling:
350 g (12 oz) potatoes
salt

1 tablespoon margarine
1 medium-sized onion, peeled
   and finely chopped
1 clove of garlic, crushed
2 teaspoons ground coriander
½ teaspoon chilli powder
1 teaspoon garam masala
2 teaspoons lemon juice
deep oil or fat for frying

Sift the flour and a pinch of salt into a bowl. Add the margarine and yogurt or curds and mix gently to a soft dough. Turn on to a floured surface and knead lightly until smooth. Shape into a ball, put on a working surface, cover with a bowl and leave to rest for 30 minutes. Peel the potatoes and cook in boiling salted water until tender. Drain well and mash. Melt the margarine in a pan and gently fry the onion and garlic with the coriander, chilli powder and garam masala for 5 minutes. Remove from the heat, add the mashed potatoes and lemon juice and mix well. Allow to cool. Roll the dough out thinly and cut into 6.5 cm (2½ inch) squares. Put a spoonful of stuffing on each square, brush the edges with a little water, then fold each square into a triangle, so that the filling is completely enclosed. Fry, a few at a time, in deep fat or oil until golden brown, remove from the pan and dry well on kitchen paper. *Makes about 20*

Grilled Celery and Bacon

It is not necessary to write a proper recipe for this as it is so simple. All you have to do is to cut some sticks of celery (choose the inside sticks if possible) into 2.5 cm (1 inch) lengths. Take as many rashers of streaky bacon as you have sticks of celery (but this obviously depends slightly on the size of the sticks of celery and the bacon rashers), cut off the rind and stretch on a board with the back of a knife. Spread with some French mustard, then cut into lengths long enough to wrap round the celery. Wrap each piece of celery in a piece of bacon and then thread on to skewers, leaving some space between each one so that the bacon can become crispy. Put under a moderate grill and cook, turning once, until the bacon is crispy. Remove from the skewers, and place on a serving plate with a cocktail stick in each piece. The flavours go extremely well together and the contrast in textures is very pleasant.

Speedy Cheese Dip

This dip will only take a few minutes to prepare, but if possible you should make it up at least an hour before serving for the flavours to infuse.

½ bunch watercress
225 g (8 oz) cottage cheese
1 clove of garlic, crushed

3 tablespoons soured cream
salt and freshly milled black pepper

Trim off about 1.5 cm (½ inch) of the stalk of the watercress, then chop the remainder very finely. Put into a basin and add the remaining ingredients. Mix together and season well with salt and pepper. Cover the dip and chill until ready to serve, as if it is left for too long in a warm atmosphere the cheese becomes rather runny. *Serves about 15*

Devilled Ham Dip

225 g (8 oz) curd cheese
2 tablespoons mayonnaise
½ small onion, peeled and
very finely chopped
50 g (2 oz) ham, very finely
chopped

few drops Tabasco
salt and freshly milled black
pepper
1 tablespoon chopped parsley

Turn the cheese into a basin and beat in the mayonnaise. Add all the remaining ingredients and leave for at least 1 hour before serving for the flavours to infuse. *Serves 15*

Avocado Dip

This may sound rather extravagant, but you can quite often buy slightly over-ripe avocados cheaply which are ideal for this.

1 small avocado pear
1 tablespoon lemon juice
3 tablespoons mayonnaise

1 tablespoon very finely
chopped onion
salt and freshly milled black
pepper

Peel the avocado pear, remove the stone and mash with the lemon juice to preserve the colour. Beat in the mayonnaise and onion and season to taste with the salt and pepper. Turn into a small serving dish, cover with cling-wrap to help preserve the colour, and chill until ready to serve. *Serves 12*

Teenage Parties

As I don't have any teenage children, before starting this chapter I consulted friends who do, to find out the sort of food their children like. The immediate reply was sausages, hamburgers and pizzas, and while I didn't consider this to be a very inspiring choice I have duly obliged with some recipes and ideas which I hope will help some parents. The other point they made was that the children hated 'fussy' food, so I have deliberately chosen food which is simple, but tasty, such as Super Special Cottage Pie, Jenny's Sausagemeat Plait and Turkey and Brown Rice Risotto.

They are not terribly 'smart' dishes, but teenage parties generally seem to be fairly casual affairs, and as I am sure I don't have to remind mothers who have children of this age, most of them have rapacious appetites. The boys in particular seem to be able to put away quantities of food, and still remain very slim, although some of the girls are very figure-conscious. All the dishes in this chapter are therefore very substantial and filling, but to make sure they don't go hungry I would suggest plenty of garlic bread (page 158), fresh wholemeal (more filling than white) and French bread, and baked potatoes in their jackets as well as plenty of salads.

When it comes to desserts, several of those in Buffet Parties would be very suitable, such as the Meringue Cake, Caroline's Plum Flan and Damson and Apple Snow.

Party Pizzas

Making up a number of small pizzas is a laborious business, so I have suggested making large rectangular ones, about 32.5 x 27.5 cm (13 x 11 inches) on a baking sheet, and then cutting them into four very generous, or six good-sized pieces. You can bake them in advance and reheat them, or you can completely prepare them prior to baking and freeze, then remove from the freezer, leave to prove and then bake. If you wanted, you could make a variety of different toppings, adding anchovy fillets, sliced mushrooms, small pieces of frankfurter, different cheeses, etc.

450 g (1 lb) yeast dough as the recipe for Bread Pasties (pages 179–81)
2 tablespoons oil
2 large onions, peeled and finely chopped
3 cloves of garlic, crushed
794 g (1 lb 12 oz) and a 400 g (14 oz) can tomatoes

salt and freshly milled black pepper
150 g (6 oz) thinly sliced garlic sausage or salami
3 teaspoons dried oregano or marjoram
225 g (8 oz) strong Cheddar cheese, grated
25 g (1 oz) stuffed olives, halved

Make up the dough as the recipe on page 180. Leave to prove until the dough has doubled in size, then divide in half and roll out to two rectangles approx 32.5 x 27.5 cm (13 x 11 inches) and making a slight ridge round the edges to enclose the filling.

While the dough is proving for the first time, heat the oil in a pan and gently fry the onions and garlic for 5 minutes. Add the tomatoes, together with the juice from the cans and seasoning. Bring to the boil, then simmer uncovered over a moderate heat for about 30 minutes, stirring frequently to prevent the mixture from sticking to the bottom, until it is quite thick. Remove from the heat and allow to cool.

Divide the tomato mixture between the two pieces of

dough and spread evenly. Top with the garlic sausage or
salami, then sprinkle over the grated cheese and decorate
with the olives. Cover with pieces of lightly oiled cling-wrap
and leave to rise in a warm place until the dough has doubled
in size. Bake in a hot oven, 220°C (425°F), Gas Mark 7 for
about 30 minutes, or until the dough is golden and the cheese
is lightly browned. If baking in advance and reheating transfer
to a cooling rack, so that the underneath of the dough does
not become soggy. *Serves 8 to 12*

Burgers and Bits

Although I find them incredibly boring, I am reliably
informed that hamburgers are almost an essential at parties
for this age group. You must use a good quality mince for this,
so unless you know that the mince from your butcher or
supermarket is good, it is safer to buy some good stewing or
braising meat and mince it yourself. You can, however,
stretch the meat by adding breadcrumbs to it (or soya protein), but make sure you season it really well with plenty of
salt and pepper. I also like to give the burgers extra flavour by
adding mustard, Worcestershire sauce, crushed garlic and
some chopped herbs, but you can of course omit these.

When you are catering for a crowd it is obviously imposs-
ible to grill or fry them all just at the last minute, but you can
keep them warm in a cool oven. First cook a batch of fairly
well done burgers, then cook some rare ones and put them
into a separate container. (If you are going to keep them
warm for more than about 15 minutes, you should make them
very rare, as they will continue cooking slightly in the oven.)
Fried onion rings can also be kept warm in the oven, as can
toasted baps, then to assemble the burgers you really need
two or three people to set up a fast-moving production line.

The relishes are all-important, but bought ones can work
out very expensive, so I have suggested some fairly quick and
easy ones you can make yourself. In addition to these you can
also have some thinly sliced tomatoes (when cheap), finely

chopped raw onion, tomato ketchup (if you add some mustard and a few chopped chives or spring onions it will jazz it up a bit), any home-made tomato or apple chutneys you have in the cupboard, some finely chopped diced cucumber mixed with some natural yogurt, etc.

900 g (2 lb) lean minced beef
150 g (6 oz) fresh white
  breadcrumbs
3 eggs, beaten
2 cloves of garlic, crushed
2 tablespoons Worcestershire
  sauce

1 tablespoon made mustard
½ teaspoon dried thyme
salt and freshly milled black
  pepper
12 baps

Put the beef into a bowl, add the breadcrumbs, eggs, garlic, Worcestershire sauce, mustard and thyme and season well with salt and pepper. Mix all the ingredients well together and beat for about 2 minutes. Form into 12 flat cakes, place on a large baking sheet and chill in the fridge for about 1 hour before cooking (or more if this is easier). Grill or fry the hamburgers, allowing about 2 minutes on each side for rare burgers and 3 to 4 minutes for well done. Toast the baps and put a burger into each bap together with some relishes, crisp lettuce leaves and fried onion rings, if wished.
  Makes 12

Corn and Gherkin Relish

326 g (12 oz) can sweetcorn
  kernels
1 large onion, peeled and
  finely chopped

2 tablespoons vinegar
2 large dill cucumbers, finely
  chopped

Drain the corn and put into a bowl. Add all the remaining ingredients, mix well and leave overnight for the flavours to infuse.

Tomato and Celery Relish

450 g (1 lb) tomatoes, peeled
  and chopped
1 medium-sized onion, peeled
  and finely chopped
2 sticks celery, finely chopped

2 level tablespoons soft
  brown sugar
3 tablespoons vinegar
salt and freshly milled black
  pepper

Put all the ingredients into a pan and bring to the boil. Reduce
the heat and simmer over a moderate heat in an open pan for
about 30 minutes, stirring from time to time to prevent the
mixture from sticking to the bottom, until it is quite thick.
Remove from the heat and allow to cool.

Green Pepper Relish

1 tablespoon oil
2 medium-sized onions,
  peeled and chopped
2 green peppers, seeded and
  finely chopped

½ teaspoon ground coriander
2 teaspoons vinegar
¼ teaspoon chilli powder

Heat the oil in a pan and gently fry the onions and peppers for
5 minutes. Add the remaining ingredients, cover the pan and
simmer gently for a further 5 minutes. Remove from the heat
and allow to cool.

Sausages and Sauces

Sausages seem to be universally popular with this age group,
and whilst, like everything else, they have risen in price, they
are still pretty good value for money. You can serve them
either with traditional old mash, baked potatoes in their jackets (much easier) or garlic bread (page 158), and I would
suggest a coleslaw salad (pages 94–5) though you could obviously serve any other salad you preferred. Allow 2 to 3 sausages per person, and if you serve all the sauces below you will

have enough for about 30. For cooking a large number of sausages, by far the easiest method is to put them into a large roasting dish and cook them in a moderate oven, 180°C (350°F), Gas Mark 4, for about 20 minutes. You can then cover them with foil, lower the heat of the oven right down to 110°C (225°F), Gas Mark ¼ and leave them until required.

Creamy Tomato Dip

1.5 dl (¼ pint) soured cream
2 tablespoons tomato ketchup
2 tablespoons mayonnaise
1 teaspoon Worcestershire
  sauce
1 teaspoon made mustard
salt and freshly milled black
  pepper

Mix all the ingredients together, seasoning to taste with salt and pepper.

Curry Mayonnaise

1.5 dl (¼ pint) mayonnaise
2 teaspoons lemon juice
1 tablespoon curry powder
2 teaspoons chutney or sweet
  pickle

Mix all the ingredients together and leave for at least 1 hour before serving for the flavours to infuse.

Yogurt and Blue Cheese

1.5 dl (¼ pint) natural yogurt
50 g (2 oz) Danish blue
  cheese, crumbled
salt and freshly milled black
  pepper

Mix all the ingredients together.

Sweet and Sour Sauce

1 tablespoon oil
1 large onion, peeled and
  finely chopped
1 clove of garlic, crushed
3 tablespoons tomato purée
1.5 dl (¼ pint) water
1 tablespoon soft brown
  sugar

1 tablespoon vinegar
2 teaspoons Worcestershire
  sauce
1 teaspoon made mustard
a good pinch of dried mixed
  herbs
salt and freshly milled black
  pepper

Heat the oil in a small pan and gently fry the onion and garlic until soft. Add all the remaining ingredients, bring to the boil and simmer gently for 5 minutes. Season to taste before serving.

Apple and Horseradish

450 g (1 lb) cooking apples,
  peeled, cored and chopped
2 tablespoons water

1 teaspoon sugar
3 teaspoons horseradish
  sauce

Put the apples, water and sugar into a small pan, cover, bring to the boil and cook until the apples are reduced to a purée. Remove from the heat, beat until the apples are smooth, then beat in the horseradish sauce. Serve either hot or cold.

Rice Cacciatori

This makes a pleasant change from interminable Spaghetti Bolognese: the sauce is basically a Bolognese sauce, but it is served with a rice pilaf. Both the rice and the sauce can be made in advance and just reheated, but do not combine them until shortly before serving.

For the sauce:

3 tablespoons oil
4 rashers streaky bacon, de-
  rinded and chopped
3 large onions, peeled and
  chopped
3 cloves of garlic, crushed
900 g (2 lb) minced beef
794 g (1 lb 12 oz) can
  tomatoes
2 tablespoons tomato purée
1 teaspoon dried mixed herbs
salt and freshly milled black
  pepper

For the rice:

3 tablespoons oil
2 medium-sized onions,
  peeled and chopped
2 green peppers, seeded and
  chopped
450 g (1 lb) long-grain rice
1.2 litres (2 pints) water
2 chicken stock cubes
100 g (4 oz) salted peanuts
salt and freshly milled black
  pepper

Heat the oil for the meat sauce in a pan and fry the bacon, onions, and garlic for 5 minutes. Add the meat and cook for a further 5 minutes. Stir in the remaining ingredients, cover and simmer gently for 1 hour. For the rice, heat the oil in a pan and fry the onions and peppers for about 10 minutes. Add the rice and stir over a gentle heat for a couple of minutes. Pour in the water and crumble in the stock cubes. Stir, cover and cook over a gentle heat for about 15 minutes or until all the liquid is absorbed by the rice. Add the peanuts, mix well and season to taste. Turn the rice on to a heated serving plate and pour over the meat sauce. *Serves 10 to 12*

Skordalia with Crudités

Skordalia is a Greek garlic sauce, not unlike Provençal aioli, but using potatoes rather than egg yolks as a base for the oil, and therefore not as rich. Ground almonds are often added as well, but I have omitted these as they are so expensive. A true Skordalia should be made with olive oil, but you can perfectly well use a corn or vegetable oil or, very often, I use half olive and half a cheaper oil. It looks very attractive for a summer party surrounded by pieces of fresh vegetable: carrot and cucumber sticks, raw mushrooms, cauliflower or broccoli florets, pieces of celery, strips of pepper, etc.

450 g (1 lb) potatoes
salt
3 cloves of garlic, crushed

1.75 dl (generous ¼ pint) oil
juice of 2 lemons
freshly milled black pepper

Scrub the potatoes and cook in boiling salted water until tender. Drain and, when cool enough to handle, peel and sieve. Add the garlic and pound into the potatoes, using a wooden spoon. Add the oil and lemon juice alternately, a little at a time, beating well until you have a smooth sauce. Season to taste with salt and pepper and serve as above.   *Serves 8 to 10*

Devilled Chicken Wings

There is not a great deal of meat on a chicken wing, but they are quite fun to eat, provided of course you expect people to pick them up and eat with their fingers. If you wished, you could complete the cooking of them over a barbecue.

20 chicken wings
6 tablespoons tomato purée
3 dl (½ pint) water
3 cloves of garlic, crushed
5 cm (2 inch) piece of root
   ginger, peeled and very
   finely chopped

1 teaspoon chilli powder
1 tablespoon ground coriander
3 tablespoons soy sauce

Place the chicken wings in a large roasting tin. Mix all the remaining ingredients together and pour over the chicken. Cover with foil and leave to marinate for about 6 hours, turning and basting from time to time. Keeping the tin covered, cook the chicken in a moderately hot oven, 200°C (400°F), Gas Mark 6, for 20 minutes. Remove the cover, baste all the joints with the sauce and continue cooking for a further 10 to 15 minutes or until the chicken wings are quite tender. Serve hot, together with the juices in the pan, with baked jacket potatoes and a tossed green salad. *Serves 8 to 10*

Super Special Shepherd's Pie

This may sound a bit humble for a party, but it usually proves popular and is wonderfully easy for Mum to prepare. You can either make it two or three days before and keep it covered in the fridge, or it will deep freeze well. I make it in a couple of roasting tins and if they are a bit old and scruffy, you can always line them completely (inside and out) with foil which will hide a multitude of sins. If you prefer you can of course use instant mashed potato, rather than boil and mash your own, but this does work out more expensive.

1.2 kg (3 lb) minced beef
650 g (1½ lb) onions, peeled and chopped
2 large green peppers, seeded and chopped
50 g (2 oz) flour
794 g (1 lb 12 oz) can tomatoes

794 g (1 lb 12 oz) can baked beans
3 teaspoons mixed dried herbs
salt and freshly milled black pepper
2.25 kg (5 lb) potatoes
150 g (6 oz) margarine
about 2 dl (scant ⅓ pint) milk

Put the beef into a large pan and fry gently, without any fat, for about 5 minutes or until browned. Add the onions and peppers and fry for a further 5 to 10 minutes. Stir in the flour and cook for 1 minute, then add the tomatoes, baked beans, herbs and seasoning. Cover the pan and simmer very gently for 1 hour. Turn into two ovenproof dishes or roasting tins approximately 27.5 x 22.5 cm (11 x 9 inches) and leave to cool. Peel the potatoes and cook in boiling salted water until tender. Drain well and mash with 100g (4 oz) of the margarine and enough milk to give a consistency which will spread easily. Season to taste with salt and pepper and spread over the meat. Make a pattern on the top, either using a fork or the point of a round-bladed knife, and dot with the remaining margarine. Bake in a moderately hot oven, 200°C (400°F), Gas Mark 6 for about 30 minutes or until the top of the potato is golden brown. *Serves 16*

Spanish Vegetable Flan

The basil in this flan gives it an excellent flavour without being too dominant, and it is filling without being heavy.

250 g (10 oz) shortcrust pastry (page 187)
900 g (2 lb) leeks
25 g (1 oz) butter
salt and freshly milled black pepper
450 g (1 lb) cooked potatoes, sliced
225 g (8 oz) cheese, grated
450 g (1 lb) tomatoes, peeled and sliced
1 teaspoon dried basil
4 tablespoons single cream

Roll out the pastry and use to line a 25 cm (10 inch) flan ring or tin. Prick the base and fill the centre with greaseproof paper and baking beans. Bake blind in a moderately hot oven, 200°C (400°F), Gas Mark 6, for 15 minutes. Remove the greaseproof paper and beans and bake for a further 5 minutes to dry out the base.

Trim the leeks, wash them thoroughly, then cut into 1.5 cm (½ inch) pieces. Melt the butter in a pan, add the leeks and fry gently for 10 to 15 minutes until they are just tender. Remove from the heat and season with salt and pepper. Place two-thirds of the potato in the base of the flan case, season and top with the leeks. Sprinkle with two-thirds of the cheese and then cover with the tomatoes, season, sprinkle over the basil, then pour over the cream. Arrange the remaining potatoes round the edge in overlapping slices. Season and sprinkle with the remaining cheese. Bake in a hot oven for about 20 minutes or until the top is golden brown. *Serves 6 to 8*

Pork and Black Eye Peas

Black eye peas (or beans as they are really) are always described as being robust and earthy, which I think is a good description of this dish.

450 g (1 lb) black eye peas	1 tablespoon dried mixed
1.8 kg (4 lb) salt pork belly	herbs
2 x 794 g (1 lb 12 oz) cans	4 cloves of garlic, crushed
tomatoes	salt and freshly milled black
900 g (2 lb) onions, peeled	pepper
and chopped	9 dl (1½ pints) stock

Put the peas and pork into separate bowls, cover with cold water and leave to soak overnight. Drain the peas and put into a large casserole. Cut the pork into 2.5 cm (1 inch) dice and add to the casserole with the tomatoes, onions, herbs, garlic and seasoning. Pour over the stock. Cover the casserole and cook in a slow oven, 150°C (300°F), Gas Mark 2 for 3 hours. Taste and adjust the seasoning before serving. *Serves 10*

Jenny's Sausage Plait

A friend of mine who has three teenage children gave me this recipe. She tells me that her children always complain about sausage rolls at parties, saying that there is too much pastry and not enough filling. I have suggested adding onions, mustard and sweet pickle to the sausagemeat, but she just adds whatever she happens to have in her cupboards which she thinks will improve the flavour, so you can obviously vary the filling to suit yourself. She says she also takes it for picnics to rugger matches when they want some hot food. Bake it shortly before you plan to leave home (you can get it completely prepared ready for baking the day before if you wish), remove it from the oven and wrap quickly in double thickness foil and then in a clean tea towel and it will stay warm for a couple of hours.

650 g (1½ lb) sausagemeat
2 medium-sized onions,
peeled and finely chopped
2 teaspoons made mustard
1 tablespoon sweet pickle
1 teaspoon dried mixed herbs

225 g (8 oz) puff pastry (page 188) or use a 398 g (14 oz) packet frozen puff pastry, thawed
a little beaten egg or milk to glaze

Put the sausagemeat into a bowl and add the onions, mustard, pickle and herbs and mix well. Roll out the pastry to a rectangle, approximately 25 x 30 cm (10 x 12 inches) and trim the edges. Mark the pastry into three lengthwise and spread the sausagemeat down the centre section. Make diagonal cuts 2.5 cm (1 inch) apart along the uncovered pastry at each side to within 1.5 cm (½ inch) of the filling. Brush the pastry strips with egg or milk and plait over the sausagemeat. Brush all over with beaten egg or milk and bake in a moderately hot oven, 200°C (400°F), Gas Mark 6, for about 30 to 40 minutes or until the pastry is golden brown. Serve hot.   *Serves 8 to 10*

Brown Rice Turkey Risotto

This is ideal for post-Christmas parties when you still have plenty of turkey to use up, otherwise you can buy a small turkey and roast it – you will need a 2.7 kg (6 lb) turkey to give you 900 g (2 lb) cooked meat. It is not the most aesthetically pleasing dish, as brown rice does not fluff up in the same way as white rice does, but the flavour is excellent and the brown rice gives it a kind of nuttiness.

100 g (4 oz) margarine	900 g (2 lb) cooked turkey,
900 g (2 lb) onions, peeled	chopped
and chopped	100 g (4 oz) sliced Danish
900 g (2 lb) brown rice	salami, chopped
1.2 litres (2 pints) chicken or	salt and freshly milled black
turkey stock	pepper
900 g (2 lb) frozen mixed	
vegetables	

Heat the margarine in a large pan and fry the onions for 10 minutes or until soft. Add the rice to the pan and toss lightly for 2 to 3 minutes. Pour over the stock, cover the pan and bring to the boil. Simmer gently for 30 minutes, then add the vegetables and cook for a further 20 to 30 minutes or until the rice and vegetables are tender; the cooking time will depend on the rice and whether the vegetables are frozen when you add them to the pan. Add the turkey and salami, cover and cook for a further 5 to 10 minutes or until the meat is thoroughly heated through. Taste and adjust the seasoning before piling on to a large platter. *Serves 15*

Children's Parties

If you are not very careful children's parties can be financially ruinous; quite apart from all the food they eat, or take and leave on their plates, or just generally scatter round the room, there are all those prizes, going-home presents and, if you are really unlucky, an entertainer into the bargain. One marvellous idea which a friend of mine had was to give all the children a large sheet of rice paper. In the middle of a large table she put some reasonably thick glacé icing, some ice cream wafers and a whole mass of cake decorations of different colours. The children then had to make a picture out of all the ingredients given, sticking the bits down with icing, spread with a teaspoon. It kept them all amused for hours: the best one was presented with a prize, and their great art efforts, served as a very good going-home present as they were edible.

Unfortunately I don't have a wealth of similarly brilliant ideas for amusing children, other than suggesting you give them all some biscuit dough and make them cut imaginative shapes out of it, or make them create some beautiful shapes and sculptures out of bread dough. I find this a marvellous way of amusing my children on a wet afternoon and if you use a packet of one of the excellent bread mixes on the market, it does not need an initial 'proving': all you have to do is add warm water to it, then knead it for 5 minutes, and no matter how much they hit it, bump it, or attempt to re-shape it, it always seems to rise up beautifully and taste very good.

As far as prizes or going-home presents are concerned, you could perhaps cut down on the cost of them by making your own fudge, and giving the winner of musical bumps, statues, etc. a square of fudge as a prize. You can also make up a big batch of shortbread-type biscuit dough (pages 140–1), cut out rings and bake them. When they are cold decorate them prettily with glacé icing and pipe each child's name on a biscuit, so that they can take it when they leave the house.

In the summer, barbecue lunch parties seem to be very popular with the over-fives, and you certainly do not need an entertainer then, as they can be organized into team and individual sports, providing of course it doesn't pour with rain. You may find some good ideas for this in the chapters on Barbecues and Teenage Parties on pages 156 and 111. One word of advice though, children's eyes are all too often bigger than their stomachs, so you are better off making small hamburgers, using chipolata sausages and buying small round rolls and bridge rolls, etc. Although it may be a bit more of a hassle to cook, it does mean that the children who really want two or three can have them, whilst the non-eaters can just have one, and with any luck you will not afterwards find yourself with platefuls of half-eaten food which always upsets the Scot in me, especially now I don't have an ever-hungry dog to feed.

However, no matter what time of the day the party is, the focal point is always, of course, the birthday cake. I have to admit that beautifully iced and decorated birthday cakes are not my forte, and whilst I battle away making trains, Snoopys, castles, etc., the funnel of the train is always crooked, Snoopy's eyes are always wobbly and the walls of my castle will generally fall at the merest touch of wind, let alone a full-scale invasion. However, the children rarely seem to notice these flaws, or if they do are far too polite to mention it, especially if they have watched one toiling over it for hours, and if I am really too embarrassed about it for the adults to see, I hide it away until all the parents have safely delivered their children and then whisk it out of the cupboard! You can therefore be safely assured that the novelty birthday cakes I have given here, are not only economical, but also *extremely* easy.

Hot Dog Twists

These are amazingly filling, so you will find a few of them go a very long way.

100 g (4 oz) quick rough puff   8 frankfurters
  pastry (page 188)   milk or a little egg to glaze
2 teaspoons French mustard

Roll out the pastry to a rectangle, approximately 30 x 15 cm (12 x 6) inches and spread with the mustard. Cut lengthwise into 8 strips and wrap a strip of pastry round each frankfurter. Place on a baking sheet, brush with milk or beaten egg and bake in a hot oven, 220°C (425°F), Gas Mark 7 for about 10 minutes, or until the pastry is just browned; do not over-cook or the hot dogs will become shrivelled and split. Serve either hot or cold, and cut each one in half or into three.   *Makes 16 to 24*

Mini Pizzas

These should appeal to the 8 to 10 year olds, either for lunch or tea parties. I have deliberately kept the topping very simple, although some children in this age group do have more sophisticated palates and enjoy stuffed olives, etc. which you can of course add if you wish.

2 tablespoons oil
1 large onion, peeled and
  finely chopped
794 g (1 lb 12 oz) can
  tomatoes
2 teaspoons dried marjoram
  or oregano
salt and freshly milled black
  pepper
350 g (12 oz) cold cooked
  sausages, thinly sliced

150 g (6 oz) Cheddar cheese,
  grated

For the dough:
350 g (12 oz) self-raising
  flour
1 teaspoon salt
75 g (3 oz) margarine
2.25 dl (generous ¼ pint)
  milk

Heat the oil in a large pan, add the onion and fry for 5 minutes. Add the tomatoes and marjoram or oregano, season and cook over a moderate heat in an open pan for about 30 minutes, until the mixture is quite thick. Stir frequently while the tomatoes are cooking to prevent the mixture from sticking to the bottom. Taste and adjust the seasoning, then allow the tomato mixture to cool.

Sift the flour and salt for the dough. Rub in the margarine, then bind with the milk to give a soft, but not sticky dough. Roll out the dough and cut into 12 x 9 cm(3½ inch) circles. Place on baking trays and divide the tomato mixture between them. Spread this evenly over the dough, then top with the sliced sausages and sprinkle with the cheese. Bake in a hot oven, 220°C (425°F), Gas Mark 7 for about 15 minutes or until they are well risen and the cheese is golden brown.

Makes 12

Sausagemeat and Apple Patties

Most children's parties call for sausages in some form or another. Sausagemeat is several pence a pound cheaper than sausages and you can 'stretch' it a bit further by adding grated apple to it, which gives a slightly sweet/sour flavour which most children seem to enjoy.

225 g (8 oz) sausagemeat
1 small onion, peeled and grated
150 g (6 oz) cooking apples, peeled, cored and grated

225 g (8 oz) puff pastry (page 188) or use a 398 g (14 oz) packet frozen puff pastry, thawed
beaten egg or milk to glaze

Mix the sausagemeat, onion and apple in a bowl. Roll out the puff pastry and cut into 30 x 8 cm (3¼ inch) circles. Divide the sausagemeat between the circles of pastry, putting it on one half. Brush the edges of the pastry with beaten egg or milk and fold over each circle so that the filling is completely enclosed. Seal the edges well, place on damp baking sheets and bake in a hot oven, 220°C (425°F), Gas Mark 7 for about 15 minutes until golden brown. *Makes 30*

Cheese and Marmite Twists

I live with a family of Marmite addicts who will spread it on almost anything from crumpets to scones and whilst some children do actively dislike it, I find it is generally fairly popular. I think these twists are nicest if they are served slightly warm, but they can be made well in advance and just reheated for a few minutes before serving.

225 g (8 oz) puff pastry (page 188) or use a 398 g (14 oz) packet frozen puff pastry, thawed

about 2 tablespoons Marmite 25 g (1 oz) cheese, finely grated a little milk

Roll the pastry out very thinly and cut into two rectangles, about 25 x 37.5 cm (10 x 15 inches). Warm the Marmite slightly so that it is easy to spread; you can do this quickly by putting the tablespoon into the pre-heated oven for a minute – literally. Spread one of the rectangles with the Marmite and sprinkle over the cheese. Brush the second rectangle of pastry with the milk to help it to stick, place on top of the Marmite-covered rectangle and press down lightly. Cut into thin strips, about 1 cm (just under ½ inch) wide and 12.5 cm (5 inches) long. Make two or three twists in each strip and place on damp baking sheets. Bake in a hot oven, 220°C (425°F), Gas Mark 7 for about 12 minutes or until well risen and golden brown. *Makes about 60*

My Own Special Bridge Rolls

I often think it is a good idea to let children see what they are eating in the way of sandwich fillings, so that the fish paste eaters do not end up with egg which they hate and vice versa. It is not very easy these days to find the old-fashioned, small bridge rolls, and even if you can buy some from your baker they are quite a bother to split and fill, apart from being rather expensive because of the labour entailed in making them, so I have devised a way of ending up with small bridge rolls without too much effort. All you have to do is make up the bread dough below (if you hate yeast cookery, I would recommend trying a packet of bread mix). When it has proved, simply roll it out into long ropes, about 1.5 cm (½ inch) wide and as long as your baking sheet. Leave it to prove and then bake it. When you want to use them, all you have to do is to split the long strips of bread in half horizontally, spread each long length with butter and any filling you wish, and then simply cut up into small pieces, about 6.5 cm (2½ inches) long, and put on serving plates. This recipe contains a high proportion of fat, which improves the keeping quality of the bread, so you can make the rolls a day before the party, or, of course, you could freeze them several weeks before.

1 teaspoon sugar	*450 g (1 lb) strong plain flour*
1.5 dl (¼ pint) warm milk	*1 teaspoon salt*
1.5 dl (¼ pint) warm water	*50 g (2 oz) lard or margarine*
2 teaspoons dried yeast	

Dissolve the sugar in the warm milk and water, mixed together. Sprinkle over the dried yeast and leave in a warm place for 10 minutes, or until frothy. Sift together the flour and salt. Rub in the fat. Add the yeast liquid and mix to a soft, but not sticky, dough. Turn on to a floured surface and knead for about 10 minutes, or until the dough feels smooth and elastic. Either replace in the cleaned bowl and cover with a damp cloth or piece of oiled polythene, or put into an oiled polythene bag. Leave the dough to rise until it doubles in size, about 1 hour in a warm place, 2 hours at room temperature or up to 12 hours in a fridge.

Turn the dough on to a floured surface and knead lightly to knock out all the air bubbles. Divide into about eight and with your hands roll into long ropes, about 1.5 cm (½ inch) wide and about 30 cm (12 inches) long and dredge them lightly with flour (this prevents the crust from becoming hard). Re-cover with a damp cloth or oiled polythene and leave in a warm place to rise until the dough has doubled in size. Bake in a moderately hot oven 200°C (400°F), Gas Mark 6 for about 15 minutes or until golden brown. Allow to cool on a wire rack, then store in an airtight container until required. *Makes about 96 small open bridge rolls*

Cheese Straws

I had always thought that cheese straws were strictly for adults' cocktail parties, until I brought home a batch from a photographic session recently. There were a collection of children in the house at the time, and, almost before I could look round, they had devoured the lot.

225 g (8 oz) plain flour　　*1 egg yolk*
a pinch of salt　　*2 tablespoons water*
100 g (4 oz) margarine　　*a little milk for glazing*
75 g (3 oz) strong Cheddar
　cheese, finely grated

Sift together the flour and salt. Rub in the margarine until the mixture resembles fine breadcrumbs, then add the cheese. Bind the pastry with the egg yolk and water to make a firm dough. Turn on to a lightly floured surface and knead lightly until smooth; if you have time it is a good idea to put it into the fridge to rest for about 20 minutes before rolling out. Roll out the pastry until it is about 0.75 cm (¼ inch) thick and brush all over with the milk. Cut into strips, about 1 cm (just under ½ inch) wide and about 7.5 cm (3 inches) long. Place on greased baking sheets and bake in a moderately hot oven, 200°C (400°F), Gas Mark 6 for about 12 minutes or until pale golden brown. Remove from the oven, allow to cool on the trays for 2 to 3 minutes, then cool on a wire rack. Store in an airtight container until required. *Makes about 75*

Traffic Light Biscuits

If I am honest these are a bit of a fiddle to prepare, but small children really do love them, which I feel makes it all worthwhile. To try to reduce the work to the minimum, I have suggested rolling out two pieces of dough; one stays complete for the base and the second one has all the little pieces cut out for the lights.

350 g (12 oz) plain flour
pinch of salt
225 g (8 oz) margarine
50 g (2 oz) caster sugar
1 egg, separated
about 3 tablespoons water

green jam (if available) or use
*   yellow or orange jam and*
*   green colouring*
red jam
apricot jam

Sift the flour and salt into a bowl. Rub in the margarine with your fingertips until the mixture resembles fine breadcrumbs, add the sugar, then bind with egg yolk and water to form a fairly stiff dough. Roll out two-thirds of the dough to a rectangle approximately 17.5 x 30 cm (7 x 12 inches). Along the short side cut out 6 small holes about 2 cm (¾ inch) in diameter and 0.75 cm (¼ inch) apart using either a thimble or a small cutter if you have one, or the top of a small bottle of vanilla essence will serve very well. Keeping the same distance, or a very little more, make another row of holes, and repeat this all along the dough. Add the trimmings from cutting the holes to the remaining dough, knead lightly, then roll out to a second rectangle 17.5 cm x 30 cm (7 x 12 inches). Brush this lightly all over with egg white, then carefully place the cut-out rectangle on top; the easiest way to lift this into position is by wrapping it carefully round the rolling pin. Press neatly down, then cut into strips, so that each biscuit has a line with three holes in it. Bake in a moderately hot oven, 190°C (375°F), Gas Mark 5 for about 15 to 20 minutes or until the biscuits are pale golden.

Colour some yellow or orange jam with green colouring if

you cannot buy any green jam, then make traffic lights out of the biscuits, by filling one hole in each biscuit red, the next orange and the bottom one green. *Makes about 22*

Chocolate Dominoes

Children will enjoy making these – with just a little help from you.

125 g (5 oz) plain flour
25 g (1 oz) cocoa
½ teaspoon salt
2 teaspoons baking powder
125 g (5 oz) soft brown sugar
2 eggs, separated
6 tablespoons corn oil
5 tablespoons milk

½ teaspoon vanilla essence

For the icing:
300 g (12 oz) sifted icing
  sugar
cold water
1 teaspoon cocoa

Grease a 32.5 x 22.5 cm (13 x 9 inch) swiss roll tin and line the base with greaseproof paper. Sift the flour, cocoa, salt and baking powder into a mixing bowl. Add the sugar. Blend together the egg yolks, oil, milk and vanilla essence. Pour into the centre of the dry ingredients and beat well to form a smooth batter. Whisk the egg whites until they form stiff peaks, then fold into the mixture. Turn into the prepared tin and bake in a moderately hot oven, 190°C (375°F), Gas Mark 5 for about 20 minutes, or until the top of the cake springs back when touched. Remove from the oven, allow to cool in the tin for 5 minutes, then turn out on to a wire rack and leave to cool.

When the cake is quite cold blend 225 g (8 oz) of the icing sugar with just enough water to give a thick, flowing consistency. Place the cake on a board, spread the icing over the top of the cake and leave for at least 2 hours to set. Very carefully cut the cake in half lengthways, then cut into strips approximately 2.5 cm (1 inch) wide; it is important to wipe the knife between each cut so that crumbs do not get on to the white icing, and you may find it a little easier if you first dip the knife into water before cutting.

Blend the remaining icing sugar with the cocoa and enough water to give a stiff icing, suitable for piping. Put the icing into a bag with a thick writing pipe, or into a greaseproof bag and simply cut off the end. Pipe lines across the centre of each rectangle and dots for the numbers to represent dominoes. Leave to set before serving. *Makes 24*

Pear Mice

No marks for originality with this recipe, but there is always a new batch of small children who will appreciate it. If you can buy cooking pears cheaply, this will obviously work out more economical than a can of pears. Simply peel them, cut them in half and remove the cores and poach in a light sugar syrup until they are just tender and then leave to cool. Now that pretty disposable jelly cases have become so expensive, I put the little mice on saucers, which is just enough jelly for most children.

2 packets lime jelly *flaked almonds*
794 g (1 lb 12 oz) can pears *angelica*

Drain the juice from the can of pears. Make up the jelly according to the instructions on the packet, using the syrup from the pears and water. Divide the jelly between 12 saucers and leave to set. Turn the pears so that the small end, where the stalk was, is towards you. Use currants to make eyes and a nose, flaked almonds for the ears and long, thin strips of angelica for the tail. Place a 'mouse' on each saucer of jelly, so that it is sitting in a green field. *Makes 12*

Chocolate Biscuit Squares

This was one of my mother's great standbys, as in old-fashioned grocers you used to be able to buy broken biscuits quite cheaply. With all the biscuits coming pre-packed these days, you are unlikely to find too many packets of broken biscuits, but it is worth looking in the bottom of the basket in which many supermarkets put slightly damaged goods, for the odd packet.

100 g (4 oz) butter or mar-garine	2 tablespoons seedless raisins
75 g (3 oz) golden syrup	225 g (8 oz) mixed sweet bis-cuits crushed
25 g (1 oz) cocoa	25 chocolate buttons

Grease a 17.5 cm (7 inch) shallow, square cake tin well. Put the butter or margarine, syrup, cocoa and raisins into a pan and heat gently until the fat has melted. Remove from the heat and stir in the crushed biscuits. Press into the prepared tin and space the chocolate buttons out evenly on the top in lines of five. Leave in a cool place to set, then cut into squares, between the buttons. *Makes 25 squares*

Coconut Meringue Diamonds

I have suggested cutting these into diamonds as they do look very attractive, but you could just as easily cut them into squares or fingers if you preferred. Don't imagine though that the edges you trim off when making the diamonds will be wasted, as I am sure eager little fingers will be standing by waiting to eat them!

150 g (6 oz) shortcrust pastry (page 187)	75 g (3 oz) desiccated coconut
2 egg whites	3 tablespoons raspberry jam
100 g (4 oz) caster sugar	

Grease a 17.5 x 27.5 cm (7 x 11 inch) swiss roll tin. Roll out the pastry and use to line the base of the tin. Prick with a fork and bake in a moderate oven, 180°C (350°F), Gas Mark 4 for 10 minutes. Whisk the egg whites until they stand in soft peaks. Gradually whisk in half the sugar, a teaspoon at a time, then fold in the remaining sugar and the coconut. Spread the jam over the pastry, then spoon the meringue mixture on top and spread carefully with a palette knife. Return to the oven for about 15 minutes or until the top is golden brown. Allow to cool in the tin, then cut diagonally across the tin into strips about 5 cm (2 inches) wide. Cut diagonal lines the other way to make diamonds. *Makes about 30*

Pussy Cat Face Meringue

I would describe this as the working mum's delight, in that it requires almost no decorating on the day; you can make it one evening and leave it to cook overnight and it can be made up several days before a party. As you won't be able to stick the candles into the meringue, you will have to put them round the cake in holders, stuck into a little bit of plasticine.

5 egg whites
275 g (10 oz) caster sugar
2 teaspoons sifted cocoa
a few drops of gravy brown-
* ing*

For the butter icing:
100 g (4 oz) butter
150 g (6 oz) icing sugar
1 tablespoon cocoa
1 tablespoon boiling water

Draw the face of a cat on a piece of paper about 25 cm (10 inches) in diameter and cut it out. Take two pieces of non-stick silicone paper; this is essential, as if the meringue sticks and breaks after it is cooked you are in trouble. Using the cut-out face as a template, draw round it on to both sheets of paper. Grease them and place on greased baking trays; if you have to use a roasting tin, use it upside down.

Whisk the egg whites until they form very stiff peaks, then gradually whisk in the sugar, a teaspoon at a time, until you have a very thick meringue. It is best to do this with an electric beater, but if you are doing it by hand, only whisk in half the sugar, and fold in the remainder. Put about 4 tablespoons of the meringue on one side. Put just over half the meringue on one of the pieces of oiled paper and very carefully spread it out with a palette knife, so that you have the shape of the cat. This will be the bottom of the cake, so try to make it as smooth as possible. Put the remaining half of meringue on the other piece of paper, and spread this out again, but stopping about 1.5 cm (½ inch) in all the way round.

Colour the reserved meringue with the sifted cocoa powder and a few drops of gravy browning (this is only made of caramel and you will not be able to taste it). Put two-thirds of it into a piping bag with a plain 1 cm (just under ½ inch) nozzle and the remainder into a piping bag with a wide writing pipe. Using the large nozzle, pipe all the way round the outline of the cat, so that it is outlined in black, and make eyes, a nose and the mouth. Using the smaller pipe, draw on eyebrows, and whiskers. Bake the meringue in a very cool oven 110°C (225°F), Gas Mark ¼ for about 6 hours, or overnight. Allow to cool, then wrap in foil until required.

Beat the butter until it is soft, then beat in half the sifted icing sugar. Dissolve the cocoa powder in the water, add to the icing and beat well, then beat in the remaining sugar; if the mixture is a little too stiff to spread easily, add a little milk. Spread the butter icing all over the plain white cat, then carefully place the black and white cat on the top. *Serves 15*

Football Pitch

There is really nothing complicated about this, all you have to do is to bake a basic Victoria sandwich mixture in a rectangular tin; the one I used was a small roasting tin 30 x 25 cm (12 x 10 inches). Split it in half and fill with butter icing, to which I added some peppermint essence which seemed fairly popular, but you could keep it plain vanilla or flavour with orange or lemon rind if you preferred. Cover with thick glacé icing coloured green and pipe on white lines for the pitch. For the nets at either end I used some of the netting off a bag of oranges I had bought in the local supermarket, held in position with cocktail sticks. You can then put football players, either plastic models or made from something like Lego, on the pitch together with a ball made from a glacé cherry. Without too much difficulty you could of course convert it to a rugger pitch or a tennis court, depending on the sporting inclinations of your children, and if you wanted to be really ambitious I should think you could make it into a swimming pool.

For the cake:
350 g (12 oz) margarine
350 g (12 oz) caster sugar
6 eggs, beaten
350 g (12 oz) self-raising flour
1 teaspoon vanilla essence

For the butter icing:
100 g (4 oz) butter or margarine

150 g (6 oz) sifted icing sugar
a few drops of peppermint essence
a little milk, if necessary

For the glacé icing:
750 g (1 ¾ lb) sifted icing sugar
about 4 tablespoons water
green colouring

Cream the margarine and sugar together until light and fluffy. Gradually beat in the eggs a little at a time, adding a tablespoon of the flour if the mixture looks like curdling. Beat in the vanilla essence. Sift in the flour and fold into the mixture. Turn into a greased and floured or lined tin 30 x 25 cm (12 x 10 inches) approximately, and bake in a moderate oven, 180°C (350°F), Gas Mark 4 for about 50 minutes or until it is golden brown and the top springs back when lightly pressed. Allow to cool in the tin for 5 minutes, then turn out on to a wire rack to cool.

Cream the butter or margarine for the butter icing and gradually beat in the sifted icing sugar and peppermint essence. If the mixture is a little stiff, add a little milk so that it will spread easily. When the cake is quite cold, split it in half horizontally. Spread the butter icing over the lower half, then reassemble. Although you normally ice the top of the cake, I found it easier for this to ice the base as it had a smoother surface. Place the cake on a wire rack with a tray underneath to catch the drips.

Sift 650 g (1½ lb) of the icing sugar into a basin, beat in just over half the water, then colour with some green colouring. Gradually beat in the remainder of the water until you have a thick, coating icing. Spoon over the top of the cake, allowing it to run down the sides, and spread evenly with a palette knife, dipped in a little hot water if necessary. Leave to set.

Sift the remaining icing sugar into a clean basin and gradually beat in just enough water to give a piping consistency. Put into a piping bag with a writing pipe or into a greaseproof bag and simply cut off the end. Pipe white lines over the football pitch; if you can't remember what it looks like any child who is a football enthusiast is bound to have a book which will show you! Make the goals as above and then put suitable 'players' on the top.

Ice Cream Cakes

Ice cream cakes are always popular with children and really are so easy to make using bought ice cream. However, you really do need to have a freezer as the ice cream must be very hard before you start working with it. To prevent it from melting, it is also a good idea to chill the serving plate or cake board before you place the ice cream on it. Once you have made the cake, put it back into the freezer until just before serving.

Train

Use an Arctic Roll for the main part of the train. Place an individual swiss roll at one end for the funnel and secure with a cocktail stick. For the wheels use circular chocolate biscuits with a hole in the middle and keep these in position with chocolate fingers pushed into the roll.

Fort

Use two of the long bricks of ice cream. Cut each one in half and place on a square cake board in a square to make the sides of the fort. Put an individual swiss roll at each corner for the turrets and stick chocolate fingers all round the sides. In the courtyard you can then put toy soldiers, horses, etc.

House

Put a brick of ice cream on to a plate. From a second brick of ice cream cut a triangle for the roof. Place in position and cut some chimneys with the pieces left over. Cover the roof of the house with Smarties and use Smarties or liquorice allsorts to make windows, doors, etc.

Names

If you have children with such names as Lucy, Edward, Harriet, Thomas, etc., you can easily make cakes using their initial. Simply cut bricks or blocks of ice cream into the L or E, etc. Place on a board and decorate with sweets, chocolate powder, hundreds and thousands, etc.

Faces

Press soft scoop ice cream into a circle on a serving plate or cake board, using a plain flan ring or loose-bottomed cake tin to help give you the shape. Put into the freezer and chill, then decorate with sweets, hundreds and thousands, etc., to make a face.

Ring Cookies

I made these for going-home presents after a recent children's party and they were a huge success, or of course you could put one on each child's plate at the table so that they know where they are to sit.

*100 g (4 oz) butter or mar-
garine*
50 g (2 oz) caster sugar
150 g (6 oz) plain flour
pinch of salt

For the icing:
100 g (4 oz) sifted icing sugar
water
colouring

Cream the butter or margarine and sugar until light and fluffy.
Sift in the flour and salt, stir into the mixture and mix to a stiff
dough, with your fingers. Turn on to a floured surface and
knead well, then roll out until it is 0.75 cm (¼ inch) thick. Cut
out circles with an 8.5 cm (3½ inch) cutter, then cut out the
centre using a 4.5 cm (1¾ inch) cutter. Re-roll the dough and
cut out more circles. You should make 12 rings in all from this
quantity of dough. Place on greased baking sheets and bake in
a moderate oven, 180°C (350°F), Gas Mark 4 for about 10
minutes or until they are a pale beige colour. Remove from
the baking sheets carefully with a fish slice and leave to cool
on a wire rack.

Mix the icing sugar with enough cold water to make a stiff
piping icing, colour with either blue or red colouring. Using
either a piping bag fitted with a plain writing nozzle, or a
greaseproof icing bag with the end cut off, pipe the name of a
child on each cookie. You can just leave the biscuits plain
apart from the name or you can pipe on a pretty design as
well. Leave until the icing has set firmly, then pack into tins in
a single layer and cover tightly until required.   *Makes 12*

Teas

At the weekend my husband considers tea to be the most important meal of the day and is quite hurt if there is not a reasonable selection of cakes, biscuits, etc. Tea-time is still a great British institution and a good, fairly inexpensive way of entertaining. I have made some of my closest friends by asking their small children home for tea after school; certainly if my children do not go out, or have a friend round, for tea at least once during the week they consider the entire week to have been a total washout!

Now that so many people have started making their own bread again, there has been a great revival of interest in yeast cookery, and yeasted tea breads are not only delicious but also cheap. Yeast cookery is not difficult and the old idea that you have to hang around waiting for the dough to 'prove' has now been totally banished. You can organize the proving of the dough round your day rather than the other way: by leaving it in a warm place if you want it to prove quickly, by leaving it at room temperature if it can take its time, or, if you want it to prove really slowly, by putting it in the fridge.

Chocolate is one of the most popular flavours for both cakes and biscuits, and there are some more chocolate recipes in the chapter on Children's Parties which I am sure would also appeal to adults. The price of cocoa has, however, risen alarmingly, so I have tried not to be over-generous with the quantities of chocolate, without allowing the flavour to suffer, but in some of the recipes you may prefer to add just a little bit more than the amount suggested.

Most cakes freeze extremely well and, provided you have enough time, it really is not a great deal of extra bother to make two cakes rather than one. This also saves fuel and means that you always have a cake readily available if people turn up unexpectedly and do not have to resort to rushing to the local baker's or supermarket and buying a cake at vast expense. If you do not have a freezer, biscuits and cakes, such as gingerbread, will keep well for a couple of weeks, if stored in airtight tins.

Ian's Chocolate Cake

My mother had this recipe from a book published just after the war; it was my brother's favourite cake and there was always a great ritual about making it before he came home from school for half-terms, holidays, etc.

50 g (2 oz) soft margarine
100 g (4 oz) caster sugar
1 egg, beaten
150 g (6 oz) plain flour
a pinch of salt
2 teaspoons baking powder
1 tablespoon cocoa
4 tablespoons milk

For the icing:
50 g (2 oz) margarine
1 tablespoon cocoa
275 g (10 oz) sifted icing
  sugar
2 tablespoons hot water

Grease a 17.5 cm (7 inch) cake tin and line the base with greaseproof paper. Cream the margarine (it is important for this recipe that the margarine is very soft), then add the sugar and cream until the mixture is light and fluffy. Gradually beat in the egg a little at a time. Sift together the flour, salt, baking powder and cocoa and fold into the creamed mixture alternately with the milk. Turn into the prepared tin and bake in a moderate oven, 180°C (350°F), Gas Mark 4 for about 50 minutes or until the top springs back when lightly pressed. Allow to cool in the tin for 5 minutes, then turn out on to a wire rack to cool.

When the cake is quite cold, split into two circles. Put the margarine and cocoa into a small pan and heat gently until the margarine has melted. Remove from the heat and beat in about a third of the icing sugar, then beat in a little of the hot water and the icing sugar alternately. Beat well, and when the mixture is beginning to thicken, divide it between the two circles of cake. Spread evenly and on the top of the cake, swirl it up with a round-bladed knife or a fork to make an attractive pattern. Place on top of the lower half and leave for at least 15 minutes to set.

Apple Cake

This is a very good way of using up windfall apples (if you do this remember to use slightly more apples as you are likely to have some wastage with bruises, etc.). Although it will not keep for too long as the apples start to go mouldy, I found the flavour was improved by keeping it for a day.

450 g (1 lb) cooking apples	*grated rind and juice 1 lemon*
225 g (8 oz) self-raising flour	*2 eggs, beaten*
50 g (2 oz) margarine	*1 tablespoon milk*
100 g (4 oz) soft brown sugar	

Grease and flour a 17.5 cm (7 inch) cake tin, ideally with a loose bottom. Peel, core and thinly slice the apples and put into a bowl of cold water to prevent them from browning.

Sift the flour into a bowl and rub in the margarine. Add sugar and lemon rind and mix lightly, then add the lemon juice, eggs and milk. Mix to a soft-dropping consistency, then spoon half the cake mixture into the prepared tin.

Cover with the apple slices and then with the remaining cake mixture, spreading it as evenly as possible. Bake in a moderate oven, 180°C (350°F), Gas Mark 4 for about 1¼ hours or until the top is golden brown and the centre is thoroughly cooked. Allow to cool in the tin for 10 minutes, then cool on a wire rack.

Coffee Gâteau

A delicious gâteau to serve at a coffee morning or for tea, but one that is not difficult to eat with your fingers, so that you will not have to give everyone a fork. The quantity of fudge frosting is a little bit generous, but as I am not very adept at icing cakes I always find it much easier to have slightly too much, and any that is left over I pour into a small container, leave to set and eat as fudge.

For the cake:
225 g (8 oz) self-raising flour
1 teaspoon baking powder
150 g (6 oz) easy-creaming
  margarine
150 g (6 oz) soft brown sugar
3 eggs
2 tablespoons coffee essence

For the filling:
100 g (4 oz) margarine
225 g (8 oz) sifted icing sugar

a few drops vanilla essence
a little milk if necessary

For the fudge frosting:
50 g (2 oz) margarine
100 g (4 oz) soft brown sugar
2 tablespoons coffee essence
5 tablespoons milk
350 g (12 oz) sifted icing
  sugar
a few walnut halves

Sift the flour and baking powder into a mixing bowl. Add all the remaining ingredients and beat well for 1 minute or until thoroughly mixed. Divide the mixture between two greased and lined 17.5 cm (7 inch) sandwich tins and bake in a moderate oven, 180°C (350°F), Gas Mark 4 for about 35 minutes or until the tops spring back when lightly pressed. Allow to cool in the tins for 5 minutes, then turn out on to a wire rack and leave to cool.

When the cakes are cold, split each one in half horizontally. Cream the margarine and gradually beat in the icing sugar and vanilla essence; adding a little milk if the mixture is too stiff to spread easily. Divide the icing between three of the circles of cake, spread evenly, then reassemble and place on a wire rack, with a plate underneath to catch any drips.

Put the margarine into a saucepan with the brown sugar, coffee essence and milk. Heat gently until the margarine has melted and the sugar dissolved. Bring to the boil and boil rapidly for 2 minutes. Remove from the heat and gradually beat in the icing sugar. Beat until the frosting has cooled a little and thickened, and then spread over the top and sides of the cake using a palette knife dipped in warm water. Place some walnut halves on the top and leave to set for 1 hour before serving.

Bran Loaf

This is one of the simplest of all tea breads, and is quite delicious when sliced and spread with butter.

100 g (4 oz) All-Bran   *3 dl (½ pint) milk*
125 g (5 oz) caster sugar   *100 g (4 oz) self-raising flour*
275 g (10 oz) mixed dried
  fruit

Put the All-Bran, sugar and dried fruit into a bowl, stir in the milk, cover and leave to soak overnight. Sift in the flour and mix well. Grease a 650 g/1½lb loaf tin, turn the mixture into the prepared tin and bake in a moderate oven, 180°C (350°F), Gas Mark 4 for 1 hour. Cool in the tin for 5 minutes, then turn out on to a wire rack to cool.

Farmhouse Fruitcake

One of the most basic and simple of all fruit cakes, but one that always seems popular.

225 g (8 oz) self-raising flour *100 g (4 oz) caster sugar*
pinch salt   *275 g (10 oz) mixed dried*
½ teaspoon ground mixed   *fruit*
  spice   *1 egg, beaten*
75 g (3 oz) margarine   *about 1.5 dl (¼ pint) milk*

Grease a 17.5 cm (7 inch) round cake tin well, and line the base with greased greaseproof paper. Sift together the flour, salt and spice. Rub in the margarine until the mixture resembles fine breadcrumbs. Add the sugar and fruit and mix lightly. Add the egg and enough milk to make a mixture that will drop from the spoon when it is shaken. Turn into the prepared tin and bake in a moderately hot oven, 190°C (375°F), Gas Mark 5 for 1 hour or until the top of the cake is

golden brown and a skewer put into the centre comes out
clean. Allow to cool in the tin for 5 minutes, then turn out and
cool on a wire rack.

Wholemeal Fruit Cake

The wholemeal flour in this cake gives it a pleasant farmhouse
feel; ideally you should keep it for 2 to 3 days before eating.

375 g (12 oz) wholemeal flour	*1 tablespoon lemon juice*
1 teaspoon ground mixed spice	*3.5 dl (generous ½ pint) milk*
1½ teaspoons bicarbonate of soda	*50 g (2 oz) chopped mixed peel*
150 g (6 oz) margarine	*100 g (4 oz) sultanas*
	50 g (2 oz) currants
	150 g (6 oz) soft brown sugar

Mix the flour, spice and soda in a mixing bowl. Rub in the
margarine until the mixture resembles fine breadcrumbs. Add
the lemon juice to the milk, which will clot the milk and sour
it. Add to the dry ingredients, together with the peel, sultanas,
currants and sugar. Beat well, then cover with a cloth and
leave overnight. Turn into a greased and floured 20 cm (8
inch) cake tin and bake in a slow oven, 170°C (325°F) Gas
Mark 3 for about 1 hour 40 minutes or until a skewer inserted
into the centre of the cake comes out clean. Allow to cool in
the tin for 5 minutes, then turn out on to a wire rack and leave
until cool. When cool, wrap in foil and store until required.

One-Layer Orange Cake

If you make this cake in a large tin in a single layer there is no
need to split and fill it, and you can just top it with an orange
glacé icing. The orange rind and juice in the cake make it very
moist.

100 g (4 oz) margarine	juice ½ large orange
100 g (4 oz) caster sugar	
grated rind 1 large orange	For the icing:
2 eggs, beaten	150 g (6 oz) sifted sugar
150 g (6 oz) self-raising flour	juice ½ large orange

Grease a 22.5 cm (9 inch) cake tin and line the base with greased greaseproof paper. Cream the margarine, sugar and orange rind until light and fluffy. Gradually beat in the eggs, a little at a time, adding 1 tablespoon of the flour with the last amount of egg. Fold in half of the remaining flour, then the orange juice and then the last of the flour. Turn into the prepared tin and bake in a moderately hot oven, 190°C (375°F), Gas Mark 5 for about 25 minutes or until the cake is golden brown and springs back when lightly pressed. Allow to cool in the tin for 5 minutes, then turn out on to a wire rack.

When the cake is cold, blend the orange juice into the icing sugar until it forms a thick, smooth icing. Spread evenly over the top of the cake and leave to set.

Orange and Cinnamon Ring

This tea bread really needs to be served freshly baked, but it freezes well, so can be made in advance and frozen.

1 heaped tablespoon caster sugar	grated rind and juice 1 small orange
1 dl (scant ¼ pint) warm water	2 tablespoons apricot jam
1 teaspoon dried yeast	2 teaspoons powdered cinnamon
225 g (8 oz) plain flour	25 g (1 oz) soft brown sugar
1 teaspoon salt	

Dissolve 1 teaspoon of the caster sugar in the water. Sprinkle over the dried yeast and leave in a warm place until frothy. Sift the flour, salt and remaining caster sugar into a bowl. Add the orange rind and juice, together with the yeast mixture and mix to a soft dough, which leaves the sides of the bowl clean. Turn on to a floured surface and knead lightly for 10 minutes. Place inside a lightly oiled polythene bag and leave to rise until the dough has doubled in size. Remove from the bag and knead lightly. Roll out to a rectangle, 50 x 25 cm (20 x 10 inches). Spread with the jam and sprinkle all over with the cinnamon and brown sugar. Roll up, like a swiss roll, and form into a ring on the baking sheet, sealing the ends together. Replace inside the polythene bag and leave to rise until the dough has doubled in size. Remove the bag and bake in a moderately hot oven, 200°C (400°F), Gas Mark 6 for about 30 to 35 minutes. Remove from the baking sheet and cool on a wire tray.

Singing Hinney

A girdle cake from Northumberland, so-called because of the noise it makes when it is put on the girdle. This is a good scone-type mixture to make if you are in a hurry and do not want to go to the bother of heating up the oven; as I don't possess a girdle, I use a thick-based frying pan and find it very satisfactory.

350 g (12 oz) plain flour	25 g (1 oz) lard
50 g (2 oz) ground rice	75 g (3 oz) currants
1 teaspoon salt	50 g (2 oz) caster sugar
2 teaspoons baking powder	3 dl (½ pint) milk

Sift together the flour, ground rice, salt and baking powder. Rub in the lard with your fingertips. Add the currants and sugar, then bind with the milk to make a soft, but not sticky dough. Turn on to a floured surface and knead lightly. Grease a girdle or thick frying pan and place over a moderate heat. When the girdle is hot, put in the hinney, then lower the heat and cook for about 15 minutes; the heat must be reduced after the first few minutes or the underside will burn without the centre being cooked. Turn the hinney: if using a girdle slip on to a plate, then very carefully tilt the plate on top of the girdle; if using a frying pan tilt the frying pan over a plate so that the hinney comes out, and then slide it carefully back into the pan. Cook for a further 15 minutes on the second side and serve warm, split in two and spread with butter.

Oat and Raisin Crunchies

100 g (4 oz) margarine
50 g (2 oz) golden syrup
75 g (3 oz) soft brown sugar

225 g (8 oz) rolled oats
a good pinch of salt
50 g (2 oz) seedless raisins

Grease a 17.5 cm (7 inch) square cake tin well. Put the margarine, syrup and sugar into a pan and heat gently until the margarine has melted. Remove from the heat and stir in the oats, salt and raisins. Turn the mixture into the prepared tin and bake in a very moderate oven, 170°C (325°F), Gas Mark 3 for 30 to 40 minutes or until golden brown. Remove from the oven, allow to cool in the tin for 5 minutes, then cut into bars. Remove from the tin and finish the cooling on a wire rack. *Makes 12*

Coconut Macaroons

Genuine macaroons are of course made with ground almonds, but these made with coconut have the same sort of texture, but are considerably cheaper.

2 egg whites
75 g (3 oz) caster sugar

100 g (4 oz) desiccated coconut
6 glacé cherries, halved

Line greased baking sheets with rice paper or silicone paper. Whisk the egg whites until they are frothy; they should not be stiff. Fold in the sugar and coconut until thoroughly mixed. Put 12 spoonfuls, spaced well apart, on the baking sheets and put a half cherry in the centre of each mound. Bake in a moderately hot oven, 190°C (375°F), Gas Mark 5 for about 12 minutes or until golden brown. Remove from the oven; if using rice paper, cut round the paper, or remove from the silicone paper and allow to cook on a wire rack. *Makes 12*

Sticky Gingerbread

I usually make two of these cakes at the same time as there is really no extra work involved in doubling the mixture and they keep well, or they can be frozen. Sometimes I make one plain one and add 100 g (4 oz) raisins, sultanas or mixed dried fruit and peel to the other.

100 g (4 oz) margarine
150 g (6 oz) black treacle
50 g (2 oz) golden syrup
1.5 dl (¼ pint) milk
2 eggs, lightly beaten
225 g (8 oz) plain flour

50 g (2 oz) caster sugar
1 teaspoon ground mixed
  spice
2 teaspoons ground ginger
1 teaspoon bicarbonate of
  soda

Grease a 17.5 to 20 cm (7 to 8 inch) square tin well and line the base and sides with greased greaseproof paper. Put the margarine, treacle and syrup into a pan. Heat gently until the margarine has melted, stirring from time to time, then remove from the heat and add the milk. Allow to cool for 5 minutes, then whisk in the eggs. Sift the flour, sugar, spice, ginger and soda into a mixing bowl. Gradually pour in the treacle mixture and beat together well. Pour into the prepared tin and bake in a very moderate oven, 170°C (325°F), Gas Mark 3 for 1¼ to 1½ hours or until the cake springs back when pressed. Allow to cool in the tin for a few minutes, then turn out and allow to cool on a wire rack. When cold, wrap in greaseproof paper and then either place in an airtight tin or wrap in foil. Leave for 2 to 3 days before eating, if possible.

Ginger and Butterscotch Buns

These buns are rather like a mixture between Chelsea Buns and an Upside-down Cake – instead of being filled with currants, they are filled with mixed peel and have a sticky ginger/butterscotch topping and filling. If you wish, you can omit the ginger completely.

1 teaspoon sugar
1.5 dl (¼ pint) warm milk
2 teaspoons dried yeast
225 g (8 oz) strong plain flour
½ teaspoon salt
25 g (1 oz) margarine
1 egg, lightly beaten

For the filling and topping:
50 g (2 oz) margarine
100 g (4 oz) soft brown sugar
1 tablespoon golden syrup
1 teaspoon ground ginger
*50 g (2 oz) chopped mixed
peel*

Dissolve the sugar in milk, sprinkle over the dried yeast and leave in a warm place for about 10 minutes, or until frothy. Sift together the flour and salt. Rub in the margarine. Pour in the yeast liquid and egg and mix to a soft dough; if the dough is a little too sticky, add a little extra flour. Turn on to a lightly floured surface and knead for 10 minutes or until the dough feels smooth and elastic. Put into an oiled polythene bag or into a bowl and cover with a damp cloth. Leave to rise until the dough has doubled in size.

Put the margarine, sugar, syrup and ginger into a pan and heat gently until the margarine has melted. Remove from the heat. Grease a 17.5 cm (7 inch) square cake tin well and pour in half the ginger mixture, spreading it evenly.

Turn the dough on to a floured surface, knead for a minute, then roll out to a rectangle 35 x 22.5 cm (14 x 9 inches) and spread with the remaining ginger mixture. Sprinkle with the peel and roll up from one of the long sides, like a swiss roll. Cut into nine rolls and place in the tin on top of the ginger mixture. Cover with a damp cloth and leave to rise in a warm place until the mixture has doubled in size. Bake in a moderately hot oven, 200°C (400°F), Gas Mark 6 for 30 minutes or until the buns are golden. Remove from the oven, allow to cool in the tin for 5 minutes, then turn upside-down on to a wire rack and leave to cool. *Makes 9 buns*

Ginger Nuts

Although you can of course buy ginger nut biscuits very easily, home-made ones really are just that bit nicer, and are one of the simplest biscuits to make.

225 g (8 oz) plain flour
1 teaspoon bicarbonate of
 soda
2 teaspoons ground ginger

½ teaspoon ground mixed
 spice
100 g (4 oz) margarine
50 g (2 oz) granulated sugar
3 tablespoons golden syrup

Sift the flour, bicarbonate of soda, ginger and mixed spice into a mixing bowl. Put the margarine, sugar and syrup into a pan over a low heat until the margarine has melted. Remove from the heat, allow to cool for 5 minutes then add to the dry ingredients. Mix well and form into a soft dough. Roll the mixture into 30 small balls, and place on baking sheets, allowing plenty of space for spreading. Bake in a moderate oven, 180°C (350°F), Gas Mark 4 for about 12 minutes or until golden brown and crisp. Allow to cool on the baking sheets for a minute and then remove and cool on a wire rack. Store in an airtight container. *Makes 30*

Bitter Lemon Roll

This is a slightly more luxurious cake than most of the others in this section, but it is not too extravagant.

3 eggs
75 g (3 oz) caster sugar
75 g (3 oz) self-raising flour
extra caster sugar or cornflour
 for dredging

For the filling:
75 g (3 oz) butter or margarine

75 g (3 oz) sifted icing sugar
grated rind of 1 lemon

For the glacé icing:
100 g (4 oz) sifted icing sugar
1 tablespoon lemon juice

Grease a 32.5 x 22.5 cm (13 x 9 inch) swiss roll tin and line the base and sides with greased greaseproof paper. Whisk the eggs and sugar together until they are light and creamy and the whisk leaves a trail when it is lifted out of the mixture. Sift the flour, then fold into the mixture. Turn into the prepared tin and level off. Bake in a moderately hot oven, 200°C (400°F), Gas Mark 6 for about 10 minutes or until the cake is pale golden and springs back when lightly pressed. Turn out on to a piece of greaseproof paper dredged with caster sugar or cornflour. Trim off the edges and quickly roll up the swiss roll, keeping it wrapped in the greaseproof paper. Allow to cool.

Cream the butter, or margarine, icing sugar and lemon rind together. Unroll the swiss roll, spread with the lemon butter cream and re-roll.

Blend the icing sugar with the lemon juice to a thick flowing consistency and spoon over the top of the roll, allowing it to run down the sides. Leave to set.

Barbecues

A barbecue is one of the easiest and most relaxed ways to entertain, and as most men seem to thoroughly enjoy doing the cooking for it, it can take a great deal of the work off your shoulders. If you cook steaks, chops, chicken joints, etc., it does tend to work out rather pricey, but there is no need to use these expensive cuts of meat, as with a little care you can barbecue quite cheap meat, without having to resort to a diet of sausages and hamburgers.

Unless you are cooking a straight steak, I feel that all meat for the barbecue is vastly improved if it is marinated prior to cooking. This not only gives it plenty of flavour and, if you brush the meat with the remains of the marinade during cooking prevents it from becoming dry, but tenderises it too. The Barbecued Breast of Lamb for example really does need to be marinated for 24 hours, as this is a cheap cut of meat and the long marinading makes it very tender.

Fish is also excellent cooked over a barbecue; obviously you can barbecue any fish you like, although the oily fish such as mackerel and trout tend to be better as some of the white fish can be rather dry if cooked in this way. I have given two fish recipes, one for Japanese Style Mackerel which is a very good but simple way of making a delicious dish out of one of the cheapest fish, and Greek Fish Kebabs, which make a pleasant change from meat kebabs.

Personally I am not very keen on kebabs which have vegetables in between the meat or fish as it is difficult to judge the cooking times of all the vegetables accurately and it is all too easy to end up with charred, overcooked tomatoes and raw onions on the same skewer. However, if you like vegetables there is no reason why you cannot intersperse them with the meat or fish; ideally use whole *small* tomatoes and onions, the latter preferably parboiled to make sure they are cooked in the middle, and blanched pieces of pepper, etc.

Another important aspect of barbecueing is safety; there are as many serious burn cases from accidents with barbecues in the summer months as there are with chip pans, so here are a few basic rules. *Never* use methylated spirits for lighting a barbecue or pour it over at a later stage (even more dangerous) because you feel the fire isn't going very well. Use special charcoal-lighting jelly if available, or use an ordinary fire lighter. These have an unpleasant smell so you must leave the fire long enough for this to burn off before starting to cook the food, but it is important anyway when barbecueing to make sure the charcoal is really hot before you start cooking. Use tongs or long-handled forks for moving and turning the food on the barbecue, as fat from the meat can flare up unexpectedly and, if you are using one of the small table barbecues, do not stand right over the food if you are attending to it as it can suddenly flare up in your face. Keep a can or jug of water beside the barbecue all the time you are cooking in case the fire suddenly gets out of hand; if you are very keen on barbecueing it is worth investing in one of the small garden sprays and when it is becoming a little fierce you can then give it a very fine spray with water. When you have finished cooking, pour water over the charcoal to make sure it is thoroughly extinguished, and this also saves fuel as it dries out quite quickly and can then be re-used.

Garlic Bread

An absolute essential I feel for any barbecue, and although
you can heat it up on the edge of the barbecue, I honestly
think it is much easier to do it in the oven.

1 French loaf, about 50 cm   *freshly milled black pepper*
    (20 inches) long   *1 tablespoon chopped parsley*
100 g (4 oz) butter   *(optional)*
2 cloves of garlic, crushed

Cut the loaf, diagonally, into about 12 slices, stopping about
1.5 cm (½ inch) from the base. Cream the butter and beat in
the garlic, pepper and parsley, if using. Spread the butter on
each slice of bread. Wrap in foil and bake in a very moderate
oven 170°C (325°F), Gas Mark 3 for about 15 minutes. Serve
hot. *Serves 6*

Barbecued Breast of Lamb

Breast of lamb is one of the cheapest cuts of meat available,
but as it does tend to be rather fatty it is often disregarded.
Cooking it slowly over a barbecue draws out much of the fat
and, if the fat has a crispy outside, it does make it a great deal
more palatable. I found it extremely popular with my children
and their friends, so would especially recommend it as a cheap
thing to serve for a barbecue for kids. If you have bought a
whole lamb for the freezer, this is a very good way of using up
the breast, which I was horrified to hear some people just
throw away or give to the animals.

1 large breast of lamb   *1 medium-sized onion, peeled*
3 tablespoons vinegar   *and finely chopped*
2 tablespoons oil   *2 cloves garlic, crushed*
1 tablespoon soft brown   *2 sprigs fresh rosemary or ¼*
    sugar   *teaspoon dried rosemary*
2 tablespoons water   *salt and freshly milled black*
    pepper

Cut the lamb into individual ribs, and discard any large lumps of fat. Put into a dish. Mix all the remaining ingredients together and pour over the lamb. Leave to marinate for 24 hours, turning frequently in the marinade. Remove the meat from the marinade and cook it slowly over a barbecue; slow cooking is important as this helps to draw out all the fat and ensures that the meat is tender. When all the meat is crisp, remove from the barbecue and put into a serving dish. Heat up the remaining marinade, pour over the lamb and serve as soon as possible. *Serves 4 to 6*

Greek Fish Kebabs

Fish kebabs make a pleasant change from the more usual meat ones. It is important to use a firm-fleshed fish for this; flaky fish such as cod and haddock are not suitable as they break up too easily, so ask your fishmonger's advice. I used monkfish, but this is not always easily available, in which case dog fish or huss, or even coley, will hold together quite well.

900 g (2 lb) white fish fillet
3 lemons
1 medium-sized onion, peeled and finely chopped
2 bay leaves, crushed
1 teaspoon ground cumin
3 tablespoons oil
2 cloves of garlic, crushed
salt and freshly milled black pepper

Cut the fish into 2.5 cm (1 inch) cubes and put into a shallow dish. Squeeze the juice from 2 lemons and in a basin mix with the onion, bay leaves, cumin, oil, garlic and plenty of salt and freshly milled black pepper. Pour over the fish and leave to marinate for 1½ to 2 hours. Cut the remaining lemon into slices. Put the pieces of fish on to six skewers with the lemon slices. Brush with the remaining marinade and cook over a barbecue for about 15 minutes, basting frequently with the remains of the marinade to prevent it from becoming too dry. *Serves 6*

London Broil

Marinating meat tenderizes it and, in the case of beef skirt, will make it tender enough to grill over a barbecue.

1 piece of beef skirt, about 900 g (2 lb)	2 tablespoons oil
	4 tablespoons water
3 tablespoons Worcestershire sauce	juice of 1 lemon
	salt

Place the beef in a shallow dish. Mix together the Worcestershire sauce, oil, water, lemon juice and salt. Pour over the beef, cover and leave to marinate for 15 to 24 hours. Remove from the marinade and put over a hot charcoal barbecue (or under a grill), allowing about 8 minutes on each side for medium-rare or rather longer for well-done steak. Remove from the heat, place on a board and cut it into slices at a slight angle. Serve with any of the sauces given for serving with sausages for Teenage Parties (pages 115–17)).   *Serves 4 to 6*

Barbecued Mackerel, Japanese style

There is nothing to beat the flavour of a freshly caught mackerel cooked over charcoal, and served simply with lemon wedges. No matter how fresh the ones on the inland fishmonger's slab appear, they just do not have the same flavour as fish that has been caught literally only a few hours before, so I think they are much improved if they are marinated in this way for an hour or two before cooking.

6 mackerel, about 275 g (10 oz) each	4 tablespoons lemon juice
	4 tablespoons soy sauce
4 spring onions, chopped	

Cut off the heads and bone out the mackerel. This is nothing like as difficult as it may sound, simply split the fish from the head down to the tail along the belly. Remove and discard the intestines, then put the fish on a board so that the cut part is facing downwards. Press all the way along the backbone with the palm of your hand, then turn the fish over and pull out the bone. All the bones attached to the backbone should come away with it, but remove any which may have been left in. Place the mackerel out flat in a large shallow dish. Mix all the remaining ingredients together and pour over the mackerel. Leave to marinate for 1 to 2 hours. Remove the fish from the marinade and fold them together again so that they are like whole fish. Put over hot charcoal and grill for about 10 minutes on either side, brushing two or three times with the remainder of the marinade. *Serves 6*

Pork Kebabs

The thick end of the pork belly is generally fairly lean but is still an economical joint and can be used to make excellent kebabs.

*500 g (1¼ lb) pork belly
    from the thick end
juice of 1 large lemon
6 tablespoons oil
1 small onion, peeled and
    chopped
1 to 2 cloves of garlic,
    crushed*

*½ teaspoon dried sage
1 teaspoon French mustard
3 juniper berries, crushed
    (optional)
1 teaspoon coriander seeds,
    crushed*

Cut the pork into 2 cm (¾ inch) cubes and put into a shallow dish. Mix all the remaining ingredients together, and pour over the meat. Leave to marinate for 3 to 4 hours, turning and basting the meat several times. Remove the meat from the marinade and thread on to 4 skewers. Grill or cook over a barbecue until the meat is thoroughly cooked, about 15 minutes, turning and basting with the marinade. Serve with rice or pitta bread and a salad. *Serves 4*

Sweet 'n' Sour Bacon Chops

Although I find the price of bacon quite horrific, penny for penny it is still pretty good value when compared to other meats and bacon chops can now be found in a number of supermarkets.

425 g (15 oz) can pineapple rings
25 g (1 oz) dark brown sugar
1 tablespoon soy sauce
2 teaspoons made mustard
6 bacon chops

Strain the pineapple juice from the rings and add the sugar, soy sauce and mustard to the syrup. Pour into a small pan, bring to the boil and boil rapidly until the mixture is reduced by half. Brush all over the bacon chops, then place over a barbecue and cook for about 10 minutes, turning frequently and basting with the spicy syrup. Half-way through cooking, add the pineapple rings to the rack as well and cook these, basting with the syrup until they are golden brown. *Serves 6*

Breakfast Chops with Yogurt Sauce

A number of supermarkets now sell very thin New Zealand lamb chops, which are known as breakfast chops and are excellent for barbecues as they cook quickly.

18 to 24 breakfast chops, depending on size
3 dl (½ pint) tomato juice
2 teaspoons made mustard
1.5 dl (¼ pint) natural yogurt
1 tablespoon chopped chives
1 tablespoon chopped mint
¼ teaspoon ground cinnamon
2 cloves of garlic, crushed
salt and freshly milled black pepper

Put the chops into a shallow dish or tin. Mix all the remaining ingredients together, then pour over the chops. Leave to marinate for at least 4 hours, turning frequently. Remove the meat from the marinade and place over a hot barbecue. Cook for about 10 minutes, turning once. Serve hot with the remainder of the marinade as a sauce. *Serves 6*

Pork Belly Rashers, Indonesian Style

This is a very free adaptation of the Indonesian recipe for Saté, but it certainly makes cheap pork belly rashers taste good.

650 g (1½ lb) pork belly rashers
½ teaspoon salt
3 cloves of garlic, crushed
1 onion, peeled and finely grated
3 teaspoons dark brown sugar
3 tablespoons soy sauce
2 tablespoons water

Put the pork belly rashers into a shallow dish; mix the salt, garlic, onion, sugar, soy sauce and water together. Pour over the pork and leave to marinate for 2 hours, turning frequently. Remove the meat from the marinade, place over a hot barbecue and cook for about 15 minutes, turning frequently, and brushing with the remainder of the marinade. Serve hot. *Serves 6*

Herby Sausagemeat Kebabs

Even if you don't grow your own fresh herbs, you can usually buy them quite easily in greengrocers and supermarkets during the summer months, so it is a marvellous opportunity to experiment with jazzing up rather dull sausagemeat. I serve these kebabs in pitta bread with a tossed green salad and they are very popular with children as well as adults.

650 g (1½ lb) sausagemeat
1 medium-sized onion, peeled
  and grated
1 tablespoon freshly chopped
  thyme
3 teaspoons chopped sage

3 teaspoons chopped mar-
  joram
1 tablespoon chopped parsley
½ teaspoon ground allspice
freshly milled black pepper

Put the sausagemeat into a bowl. Add the herbs, allspice and
plenty of black pepper. Mix together thoroughly, then form
into 12 sausage shapes. Place on skewers and grill slowly over
a barbecue for about 15 minutes or until thoroughly
cooked. *Serves 6*

Spiced Orange Glazed Spareribs

This is a particularly easy dish to serve as you pre-cook the
spareribs in the oven and then just roast them on the barbecue for 10 to 15 minutes to glaze and crisp them. Buy
Chinese-style spareribs, but try to choose fairly meaty ones as
otherwise they can be all bone.

1.25 kg (3 lb) spareribs
2 tablespoons clear honey
juice of ½ lemon
juice of 2 oranges
finely grated rind of ½ orange

2 tablespoons Worcestershire
  sauce
1 teaspoon soy sauce
salt

Cut the chops into one or two bone pieces, depending on their
size, and place in a large, shallow dish. Put all the remaining
ingredients into a pan, bring to the boil and simmer for 2
minutes. Remove from the heat and allow to cool. Pour over
the chops and leave to marinate for 12 to 24 hours in a cool
place, turning them occasionally. Drain off the marinade and
reserve and place the chops in a roasting tin. Roast in a moderate oven, 180°C (350°F), Gas Mark 4 for 45 minutes. Drain
off the liquid which has formed in the pan, add to the

marinade and boil rapidly until the mixture has reduced by half.

When the chops are required, place them on a hot barbecue and brush with the marinade. Cook for 10 to 15 minutes, turning frequently and brushing with the marinade until the ribs are crisp and well glazed. Serve with a spicy barbecue sauce (page 117) and baked potatoes in their jackets.

Serves 6

Burger Kebabs

These are very easy and cheap to make as instead of using expensive cuts of beef or lamb, you use minced beef. This, however, should be good quality, and lean. They are particularly good cooked over a barbecue, but if it pours with rain they can easily be cooked under the grill.

450 g (1 lb) lean minced beef
50 g (2 oz) fresh white bread-crumbs
1 clove of garlic, crushed
1 tablespoon chopped parsley
2 teaspoons Worcestershire sauce
1 small onion, very finely chopped
salt and freshly milled black pepper
1 egg yolk
2 medium-sized onions
1 green pepper
a few bay leaves
1 tablespoon oil

Put the beef, breadcrumbs, garlic, parsley, Worcestershire sauce, onion, seasoning and egg yolk into a basin and mix together until they are thoroughly blended. Form into about 16 small balls. Peel the onions and cook them in boiling water for 8 minutes. Drain well. Cut the onions into wedges and the pepper into 2.5 cm (1 inch) squares, discarding the core and seeds. Thread the meatballs, onions, pepper and bay leaves on to 4 skewers. Brush the onions and pepper with oil and cook the kebabs over a barbecue or under a hot grill for about 10 minutes, turning them once. *Serves 4*

Picnics

Picnics are great family occasions and we often seem to go on outings with other families in the summer, and each of us contributes something towards the meal. Whilst one obviously can stick to cold chicken, ham, Scotch eggs, and so on this can become rather monotonous, and also works out quite expensive if there are four adults and half a dozen children to feed as well. When there are children involved I try to keep to fairly basic food which (one hopes) they all like, such as Herby Beef Loaf, Picnic Pie and Bread Pasties, which have ingredients with which most of them are familiar, but are also interesting for the adults to eat as well.

There are also a few times in the year when one wants to have a rather 'smart' picnic. Being a horse-racing addict I can't resist going to Ascot, but by the time I have paid for my entrance I am usually down to my last pennies as far as food for a picnic is concerned and friends always seem to expect me to provide food, if they provide the drinks, and somehow it doesn't seem right to eat mundane food at Ascot! The Smoked Salmon Mousse on page 170 is delicious, but very rich and filling, so people really can't eat very much of it and if, as I suggest, you use smoked salmon pieces it really is very inexpensive. Smoked Fish Flan and Chicken and Pork Galantine are two other fairly elegant main courses and if you want a starter, Iced Carrot Soup which you can take in a thermos flask is very good, or the Chilled Summer Soup from dinner parties on page 41.

Hot soups are marvellous winter picnic fare, or summer come to that if you are going to be sitting on a beach in a typical British summer. The puréed vegetable soups, such as Celeriac (page 169) and Brussels Sprouts (page 40) are good for this as, having no bits in, they are very easy to drink out of a mug or cup.

Although I love picnics, I am not very organized about them. Some people seem to be so efficient, always having sensible-sized plates, neat little knives and forks, and count-less small containers in which to put salads, dressings and sauces. As I imagine there are other people who find it as difficult as I do, I have deliberately given recipes for things which are easy to pack up and take, or can be taken to the picnic in the dish in which they have been cooked.

I have not given any recipes for salads, as I think you will find plenty of salad recipes in other chapters, especially in the Buffet Parties, which are eminently suitable for picnics. If you are making a green salad, you obviously cannot dress this before you leave home and must take your dressing in a small screw-topped jar, or a plastic container with a well-fitting lid (make sure you pack it upright though, as even the best-fitting lid has been known to leak all over the picnic basket if you put it in sideways). Other than that I always try to choose salads which I can prepare completely at home, such as potato salad, rice salad, coleslaw, red cabbage salad, etc.

I tend to be rather lazy about desserts, and certainly when soft fruits are in season, just take plenty of fresh fruit. How-ever, there are several recipes for flans, mousses and fools in other chapters which you could use for picnics. Old yogurt, cream and cottage cheese cartons (especially ones with lids) are very good for mousse-type desserts as not only are they easy to carry there, they are also easy to pack up and bring home again. If the weather is hot, I would avoid making any-thing which contains cream, as it can go off surprisingly quickly, and if you want to make up a dessert containing gelatine, increase the amount of gelatine by 50 per cent or you may find yourself with a very liquid pudding.

A few other useful hints: take two or three clean damp J-cloths in separate small polythene bags and you can use them not only for wiping fingers, but wiping over cutlery, etc. before packing it away again. Although it doesn't taste quite as nice, a small tin of dried milk for tea and coffee is much easier than taking fresh milk, unless you have plenty of thermos flasks. Don't forget to take a bottle opener, and finally, always remember to take your litter home!

Iced Carrot Soup

Chill the soup well before pouring it into the Thermos flask and rinse this out first with some iced water to make sure it is really cold.

25 g (1 oz) butter or mar-
    garine
450 g (1 lb) carrots, peeled or
    scraped and sliced
1 leek, cleaned and chopped
1 large onion, peeled and
    chopped

6 dl (1 pint) stock
salt and freshly milled black
    pepper
1 teaspoon sugar
4 tablespoons single cream or
    top of the milk

Heat the butter or margarine in a pan and fry the carrots, leek and onion for about 5 minutes. Add the stock and seasoning. Cover and simmer gently for about 45 minutes. Remove the pan from the heat and either rub through a sieve or put into a blender. Add the sugar and cream or top of the milk. Taste and adjust the seasoning and chill. Pour into the flask shortly before you leave home. *Serves 4 to 6*

Celeriac Soup

I find this one of my most popular winter soups and it is certainly one of my favourites.

50 g (2 oz) margarine
1 celeriac weighing about
    450 g (1 lb), peeled and
    roughly chopped
1 medium-sized potato,
    peeled and roughly chop-
    ped
1 medium-sized onion, peeled
    and chopped

1 leek, cleaned and chopped
    or use a larger onion
2 carrots, peeled and chopped
9 dl (1½ pints) stock
3 dl (½ pint) milk
salt and freshly milled black
    pepper
2 tablespoons chopped pars-
    ley

Melt the margarine in a large pan. Add the vegetables, cover and cook gently for about 15 minutes. Add the stock, milk and seasoning, bring just to the boil, then simmer gently for a further 20 minutes. Sieve the soup or put into a blender to make a smooth purée. Taste and adjust the seasoning, add the parsley and reheat to boiling point. Pour into a Thermos as soon as possible. *Serves 6 to 8*

Smoked Salmon Mousse

My fishmonger sells smoked salmon pieces incredibly cheaply, and it is worth scouting round your local shops to find a friendly supplier. Failing that you can buy frozen smoked salmon pieces which, while not as cheap, are usually about half the price of normal smoked salmon.

225 g (8 oz) smoked salmon
   pieces
225 g (8 oz) cottage cheese
juice of 1 lemon
2 teaspoons powdered
   gelatine

2 eggs, separated
1.5 dl (¼ pint) soured cream
4 tablespoons mayonnaise
freshly milled black pepper
salt, if necessary

Put the smoked salmon into a blender with the cottage cheese, switch on until you have a smooth purée, then spoon into a bowl. Pour the lemon juice into a basin, sprinkle over the gelatine and leave to soften for 5 minutes. Stand the basin over a pan of hot water and leave until the gelatine has dissolved. Remove from the heat and stir into the smoked salmon mixture with the egg yolks, soured cream and mayonnaise. Beat well and season to taste with plenty of freshly milled black pepper and salt, if necessary. Whisk the egg whites until they form stiff peaks, then fold into the mixture. Turn into a dish and chill in the fridge for at least 2 hours. *Serves 8 as an hors d'oeuvre or 6 as a main dish*

Potted Chicken and Ham

A good way of using up some end pieces of chicken and ham, this makes a good picnic starter, spread on slices of French bread or biscuits.

150 g (6 oz) cooked chicken
100 g (4 oz) cooked ham
100 g (4 oz) butter
1 teaspoon made mustard

salt and freshly milled black
pepper
¼ teaspoon grated nutmeg
a good pinch of dried thyme

Finely mince the chicken and ham. Soften 75 g (3 oz) of the butter and beat into the minced mixture. Add the mustard, seasoning, nutmeg and thyme and beat well. Turn into a pot. Melt the remaining butter and spoon over the top of the meat to seal it. Keep in the fridge until required; provided the seal is not broken it can be kept for about a week in a fridge. *Serves 8*

Smoked Fish Flan

It is best to cook this in a china or tin flan dish, rather than a flan ring on a baking sheet, so that it is easy to carry.

150 g (6 oz) shortcrust pastry
(page 187)
150 g (6 oz) smoked had-
dock, cod, whiting, etc.
1.5 dl (¼ pint) milk
1 tablespoon butter or mar-
garine

1 small onion, peeled and
finely chopped
2 eggs
100 g (4 oz) cottage cheese
salt and black pepper

Roll out the pastry and use to line a 20 cm (8 inch) deep flan tin or dish. Prick the base and fill the centre with a circle of greaseproof paper and baking beans. Bake blind in a moderately hot oven, 190°C (375°F), Gas Mark 5 for 12 minutes. Remove the greaseproof paper and beans and bake for a further 5 minutes to dry out the base.

While the case is cooking, put the fish into a pan with the milk. Cover and poach gently for about 10 minutes or until the fish is tender. Remove the fish from the milk, skin, bone and flake. Melt the butter or margarine in a small pan and gently fry the onion for 5 minutes. Remove from the heat. Beat the eggs, beat in the cheese, then the strained milk from cooking the fish and the onion. Season well with salt and pepper. Place the pieces of flaked fish in the bottom of the flan case. Pour over the cheese and egg mixture. Return to the oven and bake for about 20 minutes until the filling is set and the top is pale golden. Allow to cool.   *Serves 4 to 6*

Tuna, Rice and Mushroom Roll

I think this roll is at its best served with a garlic-flavoured mayonnaise, or a devilled mayonnaise with some mustard and Tabasco added to it.

184 g (6½ oz) can tuna	*2 teaspoons dried dill*
25 g (1 oz) butter or margarine	*salt and freshly milled black pepper*
1 medium-sized onion, peeled and finely chopped	*150 g (6 oz) quick rough puff pastry (page 188)*
100 g (4 oz) mushrooms, finely chopped	*2 hard-boiled eggs, shelled and sliced*
225 g (8 oz) cooked rice	*a little beaten egg to glaze*

Drain off the oil from the tuna into a small pan. Heat, with the butter or margarine, and fry the onion gently for 5 minutes. Add the mushrooms and continue cooking for a further 5 minutes, then remove from the heat, and stir in the rice, dill and seasoning.

Roll out the pastry to a rectangle 30 x 35 cm (12 x 14 inches). Place half the rice mixture in a band down the centre approx 10 cm (4 inches) wide, place the eggs, then tuna in a line on the top, and cover with the remainder of the rice mixture. Brush the edges with beaten egg, then bring together to form a roll, so that the filling is completely enclosed. Turn the roll over, so that the join is underneath and place on a damp baking sheet. Roll out the pastry trimmings, cut into decorations and place in position. Brush all over with beaten egg and bake in a hot oven, 220°C (425°F), Gas Mark 7 for about 40 minutes, or until golden brown all over. Remove from the oven and allow to cool.   *Serves 8*

Stuffed Streaky Bacon

For this recipe you need two whole pieces of streaky bacon weighing about 650 g (1½ lb) each (or one whole joint weighing 1.25 kilo (3 lb) and then cut it in half yourself). You can buy this from grocers where they cut their own bacon or you can do what I did, and just ask in a supermarket whether the bacon cutters upstairs could possibly cut you a joint like this, which they are generally quite happy to do.

2 joints of streaky bacon weighing about 650 g (1½ lb) each
50 g (2 oz) margarine
1 medium-sized onion, peeled and finely chopped
2 sticks celery, finely chopped
50 g (2 oz) dried apricots, chopped

100 g (4 oz) fresh white breadcrumbs
salt and freshly milled black pepper
¼ teaspoon dried basil
1 egg yolk
50 g (2 oz) dried breadcrumbs

Remove any small bones from the bacon. Put the joints into a large bowl or pan, cover with cold water and leave to soak overnight. Melt the margarine in a small pan and gently fry the onion and celery for 5 minutes. Remove from the heat, and put into a basin with the apricots, breadcrumbs, seasoning and basil. Mix together and bind with the egg yolk. Lay one of the bacon joints on a board with the skin underneath. Spread with the stuffing, and cover with the second bacon joint, skin side up. Tie in place with string. Wrap in foil and cook in a moderate oven, 180°C (350°F), Gas Mark 4 for 1½ hours. Remove from the oven and place between two boards with a weight on top to press it while it is cooling. When the bacon is quite cold, remove the string, strip off all the skin and roll in the dried breadcrumbs so that the fat is coated in crumbs. Wrap in foil to take on a picnic. *Serves 8 to 10*

Herby Beef Loaf

This meat loaf is an old favourite of mine which always proves very popular with both children and adults. You can vary it, and make it stretch for a few more people, by placing 3 hard-boiled eggs in the centre. Boil the eggs for 5 minutes only, then shell. Place half the meat mixture in the loaf tin, arrange the eggs in a line down the centre, then top with the remainder of the meat mixture. If adding the eggs it is also advisable to use a slightly larger tin, if you have one.

450 g (1 lb) lean minced beef
225 g (8 oz) pork sausagemeat
50 g (2 oz) fresh white breadcrumbs
1 onion, peeled and grated
1 tablespoon chopped parsley
1 tablespoon chopped chives

½ teaspoon freshly chopped sage
2 teaspoons Worcestershire sauce
salt and freshly milled black pepper
2 eggs, beaten

Mix all the ingredients together and bind with the beaten egg. Turn into a greased 900 g (2 lb) loaf tin and cover with foil. Stand in a roasting tin containing 2.5 cm (1 inch) of hot water and bake in a moderate oven, 180°C (350°F), Gas Mark 4 for 1½ hours. Remove from the heat and stand some weights on top of the foil to press it while it is cooling. Either turn out of the tin and wrap in foil, or leave in the tin if this makes it easier to carry. *Serves 6 to 8*

Pressed Lambs' Tongues

Lambs' tongues are quite a bit cheaper than ox tongue, but can be served in exactly the same way. This recipe also uses a knuckle of bacon to give extra flavour, as well as a small amount of extra meat.

1 bacon knuckle	3 sticks of celery, chopped
12 lambs' tongues	1 teaspoon black peppercorns
2 medium-sized onions, peeled and chopped	2 bay leaves
	few parsley stalks
3 carrots, peeled and chopped	salt

Place the knuckle in a bowl, cover with cold water and leave to soak overnight. Drain and put into a large pan. Rinse the tongues in cold water and add to the pan. Cover with fresh cold water, bring slowly to the boil and remove any scum. Add the onions, carrots, celery, peppercorns, bay leaves and parsley stalks, cover the pan and simmer very gently for 2 hours.

Remove from the heat and pour all the contents of the pan into a large sieve or colander, placed over a clean pan. Remove the knuckle, take off the meat and chop, and put the bone and skin back into the saucepan with the strained liquor. Bring to the boil and boil rapidly until the liquor is reduced by half.

Plunge the tongues into cold water and, when cool enough to handle, pull off the skins, and remove any pieces of bone and tubes. Arrange half the tongues in the base of a 17.5 cm (7 inch) cake tin and fill up the gaps in between with the pieces of bacon. Repeat with the remaining tongues and bacon.

Taste the cooking liquor and adjust the seasoning. Strain over the tongues in the cake tin, so that they are completely covered. Place a small plate on the top and put a heavy weight on top to press it firmly. Allow to cool, then place in the fridge and leave overnight. Either unmould from the tin, by placing the tin quickly in hot water and inverting it on to a plate, or carry to the picnic in the cake tin. *Serves about 10*

Picnic Pie

A good family pie, this is made with sausagemeat and bacon, which will appeal to children, but is sufficiently tasty to be popular with adults as well. For easy transportation I usually leave it in the tin in which it has been baked.

350 g (12 oz) shortcrust pastry (page 187)
450 g (1 lb) pork sausagemeat
150 g (6 oz) streaky bacon

1 large onion, peeled
50 g (2 oz) fresh white breadcrumbs
½ teaspoon dried sage
4 eggs

Lightly grease a 20 cm square x 5 cm deep (8 inch square by 2 inches deep) tin. Roll out two-thirds of the pastry and use to line the base and sides of the tin. Roll out the remainder of the pastry to a 20 cm (8 inch) square for the lid.

Put the sausagemeat into a bowl. Cut off the rind from the bacon and put through a mincer with the onion. Blend with the sausagemeat and add the breadcrumbs and sage. Put into the pastry-lined tin and hollow out 4 holes for the eggs. Break an egg into each hole. Damp the pastry edges, place the pastry lid on the pie, and seal the edges. Roll out any trimmings, cut into leaves to decorate the top and place in position. Bake in a moderately hot oven, 200°C (400°F), Gas Mark 6 for 20 minutes, then lower the heat to 180°C (350°F), Gas Mark 4 for a further 40 minutes. Remove from the oven and allow to cool. *Serves 6 to 8*

Mixed Winter Cheese Salad

Preceded by a warming soup, such as Celeriac (page 169) this makes a good winter picnic meal. It is easy to carry, as you put all the ingredients together into a large plastic container (I usually use one of those large ice cream containers) and you can just take the dressing separately in a screw-topped jar, and that is all you will need for your main course apart from some buttered French or wholemeal bread.

1 small cauliflower	225 g (8 oz) Edam cheese
225 g (8 oz) Brussels sprouts	100 g (4 oz) sliced salami,
225 g (8 oz) Chinese leaves	garlic sausage or cooked
1 box of mustard and cress	ham
1 kohlrabi (optional)	6 tablespoons French dres-
4 sticks celery	sing (page 189)

Break the cauliflower into florets. Cut off the outside leaves of the Brussels sprouts and shred. Shred the Chinese leaves and trim the mustard and cress. Peel and finely dice the kohlrabi, if using, and chop the celery. Wash all the green vegetables, dry very well and place in a plastic container. Cut the cheese and salami, garlic sausage or ham into thin matchstick pieces and add to the salad. Shortly before serving, pour over the dressing and toss very well so that every leaf is coated. *Serves 6*

Chicken and Pork Galantine

This galantine is surprisingly cheap to make, as it stretches a 1.25 kilo (3 lb) chicken into serving 8 to 10 people. I put a spicy Spanish chorizo sausage into the centre of mine, which flavours all the meat, but you could use another similar sausage, or even a large knackwurst if you preferred. Remember not to waste the chicken bones – boil them up with an onion and some herbs to make stock.

1.25 kg (3 lb) chicken
salt and freshly milled black pepper
50 g (2 oz) margarine
the chicken liver
1 medium-sized onion, peeled and chopped

450 g (1 lb) lean minced pork
100 g (4 oz) fresh white breadcrumbs
1 teaspoon dried tarragon
1 egg, beaten
1 chorizo sausage weighing about 100 g (4 oz)

Cut the chicken skin and flesh down the backbone using a sharp knife. Cut off both the leg and wing joints and gradually work the flesh away from the carcass and remove. Cut off the first joint of the wing and discard and gently scrape the meat back from the bone on the remaining joints and remove. Scrape the meat off both leg joints and remove. This is not nearly as complicated as it may sound, providing you have a little patience, and although you should try not to pierce the skin, if you do you can always sew it together again with thread.

Lay the chicken out flat on the board and season lightly with salt and pepper. Melt half the margarine in a small pan and gently fry the chicken liver for 5 minutes. Remove from the pan and chop finely. Add the onion to the fat remaining in the pan, and fry gently for 5 minutes. Put the liver, onion, pork, breadcrumbs, tarragon and plenty of seasoning into a bowl. Mix well together and bind with the beaten egg. Spread half the pork in a band about 12.5 cm (5 inches) wide down the centre of the chicken. Peel off the skin from the chorizo and place in the centre, then cover with the remaining pork mixture. Bring the edges together to form a neat parcel and sew up with coarse thread or fine string. Place in a roasting tin with the join underneath and spread the top with the remaining margarine. Season with salt and pepper and roast in a moderate oven, 180°C (350°F), Gas Mark 4 for 1½ hours. Remove from the oven and allow to cool.   *Serves 8 to 10*

Country Pâté

The three meats used to make this pâté are pig's liver, sausagemeat and a piece of bacon forehock, all of which are good value for money.

450 g (1 lb) lean bacon fore-hock
1 tablespoon clear honey
2 teaspoons soft brown sugar
4 cloves
3 peppercorns
a sprig of thyme
1 small bay leaf
1 onion
1 slice brown bread
225 g (8 oz) pig's liver

100 g (4 oz) pork sausagemeat
50 g (2 oz) lard, melted
1 clove of garlic, crushed
grated rind of ½ lemon
⅛ teaspoon ground allspice
⅛ teaspoon grated nutmeg
salt and freshly milled black pepper
1 egg, beaten
1 to 2 tablespoons dry sherry
1 large lemon

Put the bacon into a pan with the honey, sugar, cloves, peppercorns, thyme, bay leaf and enough water to cover. Cover it with a lid, bring to the boil and simmer gently for 40 minutes, then remove from the pan and take off the rind. Peel the onion, cut the crusts off the bread and mince with the bacon and liver. Add all the remaining ingredients, except the whole lemon, and beat well to blend. Cut the whole lemon into thin slices and use to line the base and sides of a 1.2 litre (2 pint) terrine or ovenproof dish. Spoon in the pâté, cover with a lid or foil and stand in a roasting tin containing 2.5 cm (1 inch) of cold water. Cook in a very moderate oven, 170°C (325°F), Gas Mark 3 for 2 hours. Remove from the oven and stand a weight on the top of the pâté while it cools. Take to the picnic and serve in the terrine or dish. *Serves 6 to 8*

Bread Pasties

This is a variation of an Italian recipe – it is similar to a pizza, but instead of having a circle of yeast dough with a topping, the equivalent of the topping is enclosed inside the dough. It makes an extremely good picnic meal, especially when you are not going to be able to give people plates and want something which you hold in your hand and eat. You can eat them cold, but if you want them warm, you can make them up the night before, then put them in the fridge to prove overnight and quickly bake them the following morning. If you wrap them up in foil and a tea-towel they will keep warm for some time.

For the dough:
1 teaspoon sugar
3 dl (½ pint) warm water
2 teaspoons dried yeast
450 g (1 lb) plain flour
1½ teaspoons salt
2 tablespoons oil

For the filling:
8 slices Danish Havarti
   cheese, 225 g (8 oz)
   approximately
100 g (4 oz) sliced Danish
   salami
450 g (1 lb) tomatoes, peeled
   and sliced
2 teaspoons dried marjoram
   or oregano
salt and freshly milled black
   pepper

Dissolve the sugar in the water, sprinkle over the dried yeast and leave for 10 minutes or until the mixture is frothy. Sift together the flour and salt. Add the yeast liquid and oil and mix to a dough which will leave the sides of the bowl clean. Turn out on to a floured working surface and knead for 10 minutes or until the dough feels smooth and elastic. Place inside a large polythene bag and leave to rise until the dough has doubled in size.

Remove the dough from the bag and knead lightly for 1 to 2 minutes. Divide into eight and roll each piece out to a 15 to 17.5 cm (6 to 7 inch) circle. Arrange a slice of cheese, topped with an eighth of the salami and tomatoes, on half of each circle. Sprinkle with a little of the herbs and season with a little salt and plenty of freshly milled black pepper. Fold over

the other half of the circle and press the edges together to
make a semicircle. Place on greased baking sheets and cover
with a sheet of lightly oiled polythene or cling-wrap. Leave to
rise until the dough has doubled in size. Bake in a hot oven
220°C (425°F), Gas Mark 7 for 15 to 20 minutes or until
golden brown.   *Makes 8*

Drinks

For most forms of entertaining the major expense is usually the booze; basically of course the booze itself is quite cheap, it is just that we have to pay vast amounts of duty on it. I was quite horrified when I was told recently that the cost of the bottle, transport and duty on wine is in the region of £1 – anything you pay over that is what you are paying for the wine.

It therefore makes sense, provided you are sufficiently enthusiastic, to make your own wine and beer on which there is no tax (remember that distilling your own gin and whisky is illegal!). Apart from the obvious shops, such as Boots, which have been selling home-brewing kits for years, some supermarkets now have quite a good range as well. The main things you need for home-brewing are a certain amount of time, some storage space and the patience to wait the required number of days and weeks for the necessary fermenting to take place. For someone like myself the last part is the hardest – if I sow seeds in the garden I rush out every day to see if they are coming through and if nothing has happened after about ten days I become quite disenchanted! At your first attempt you are unlikely to make a prize-winning brew, although it should be drinkable, but practice and experience are all-important and I have had some very pleasant evenings enjoying other people's excellent home-brew.

Punches for summer parties and gluwein for winter can both be pretty cheap ways out, and depending on the state of your purse you can lace the gluwein with brandy or add extra spirit to the punch. If you want to appear grander than you really are, you can always serve 'champagne cocktails'. Use the cheapest brandy you can buy and instead of champagne buy a sparkling white wine, such as Veuve du Vernay. In summer I find Buck's Fizz with fresh orange juice and a sparkling white wine (or the cider) goes down well. Especially if the weather is very hot and people are thirsty, you can up the quantity of orange juice and nobody notices or minds.

How much to allow is always a problem and largely depends on how boozey your friends are, but generally allow ⅓ litre or about half a bottle of wine for dinner, and for drinks and buffet parties the equivalent of about ½ litre or just over half a bottle. For a large party, you can usually buy drinks from an off-licence on a sale or return basis, and don't forget that most off-licences will lend you glasses (usually free of charge) if you are buying drinks from them.

Kir

Kir is a very refreshing French drink, but in order to make it you must have some blackcurrant liqueur called Crème de Cassis. This is not difficult to obtain from good off-licences and although a litre bottle of it may seem quite expensive you will find that it will last for a long time. Simply put about 1 teaspoon of cassis in the bottom of a wine glass, top up with chilled, dry white wine and stir lightly. To make it stretch even further you can also add a dash of soda water and a large ice cube to each glass.

Tea and Rum Punch

1 tablespoon Indian tea leaves
3 tablespoons roughly chop-
ped mint leaves
1.2 litres (2 pints) boiling
water
2 tablespoons clear honey
1 litre (1¾ pints) ginger ale

3 dl (½ pint) white rum
juice 4 large lemons

To garnish:
2 sliced lemons
few mint sprigs

Put the tea leaves and mint into a large bowl. Pour over the boiling water, stir well, then leave to infuse for 15 minutes. Put the honey into the base of a large clean jug, strain over the tea and stir well. Allow to cool, then chill thoroughly. Chill the ginger ale at the same time. Mix the rum, lemon juice and ginger ale into the tea mixture. Stir well, then add the lemons and mint sprigs. *Makes 25 glasses*

Sangria

This is a well-known Spanish drink; the fruit content is all-important as a sweetener and if you use a very dry red wine, you may find it necessary to add a little sugar.

1½ litres (2½ pints) red wine
7.5 dl (1¼ pints) lemonade

Fruit, e.g. sliced oranges,
peaches, bananas, straw-
berries, cherries, etc.

Chill the wine and lemonade thoroughly. Mix together shortly before serving and add the fruit. *Makes 20 glasses*

White Wine Cup

*1½ litres (2½ pints) dry
  white wine
1½ litres (2½ pints)
  lemonade*

*1.5 dl (¼ pint) brandy
Fruit, e.g. oranges, lemons,
  strawberries, peaches, etc.
a few ice cubes*

Chill the wine and lemonade thoroughly. Put into a punch bowl with the brandy and add plenty of fruit and a few ice cubes. *Makes 30 glasses*

Cider Buck's Fizz

This drink is at its very best when first mixed, so that there are still some bubbles from the cider in it.

*2 litres (3½ pints) dry cider
1 litre (1¾ pints) fresh
  orange juice*

*2 dl (generous ¼ pint) cheap
  brandy*

Thoroughly chill the cider and orange juice. Pour the brandy into a large jug and mix in the orange juice. Add the cider just before serving and mix well. *Makes 25 glasses*

Gluwein

*2 lemons
1 litre (1¾ pints) cheap red
  wine
scant litre (1½ pints) water
8 cloves*

*1 stick cinnamon
about 100 g (4 oz) caster
  sugar
1 dl (scant ¼ pint) cheap
  brandy*

Peel the zest thinly from the lemons. Cut a few slices of lemon for decoration, then squeeze the remaining lemon to extract the juice. Put the lemon zest, juice, wine, water, cloves and cinnamon into a pan. Put on the lid, bring to just below simmering point and leave at this temperature for 1 hour. Lift out the lemon rind, cloves and cinnamon and add sugar to taste. Add the brandy and serve hot with lemon slices floating on the top.   *Makes 16 glasses*

The Bishop

A rather 'special' Christmas drink.

2 lemons
6 cloves
½ teaspoon ground mixed
  spice
3 dl (½ pint) water
1 bottle cheap port
45 to 60 g (1½ to 2 oz) loaf
  sugar

Stick the cloves into one of the lemons. Put into a tin and bake in a moderate oven, 180°C (350°F), Gas Mark 4 for 30 minutes. Put the mixed spice into a pan with the water, bring to the boil and simmer for 5 minutes. Heat the port to just below boiling point, add the spiced water and lemon and keep warm for 20 minutes. Meanwhile rub the loaf sugar into the rind of the second lemon and squeeze the juice. Add to the punch and heat gently to dissolve the sugar.
   Makes 10 glasses

Basic Recipes

Here are just a few basic recipes to save you having to refer to another book if you can't remember the proportions for pastry, white sauce, etc. When I have referred to these recipes 3 dl (½ pint) white sauce for example means sauce using 3 dl (½ pint) milk and in pastry recipes 225 g (8 oz) shortcrust pastry means pastry made with 225 g (8 oz) flour, *not* the total weight of the pastry.

Shortcrust Pastry

225 g (8 oz) plain flour
pinch of salt
100 g (4 oz) fat: butter, or
  margarine or a mixture of
  margarine and lard

about 3 tablespoons cold
  water

Sift together the flour and salt. Cut the fat into small pieces and, using your fingertips, rub it into the flour until the mixture resembles fine breadcrumbs. Add the water, using a palette knife to cut and stir the mixture thoroughly, so that it clings together leaving the sides of the bowl clean. Put the pastry on to a floured board or working surface, and knead very lightly so that you have a smooth round ball. Roll out, and use as required.

It is very important when making shortcrust pastry to ensure that the mixture is not overhandled, and that you do not add too much water as this makes the pastry tough, and causes it to shrink considerably during the cooking. *Makes 225 g (8 oz)*

Quick Rough Puff Pastry

225 g (8 oz) plain flour
pinch of salt
75 g (3 oz) lard

75 g (3 oz) margarine
1.5 dl (¼ pint) water

Sift the flour and salt into a bowl. Add the fat and cut up roughly into 1.5 cm (½ inch) cubes using two round-bladed knives in a scissor action. Mix to a soft dough with the water. Roll out on a floured board to an oblong about 30 x 12.5 cm (12 x 5 inches). Bring the top third of the pastry down and the bottom third of the pastry up, to make an envelope shape. Turn the pastry at right angles and repeat the rolling and folding three more times. Chill for about 20 minutes, and then use as directed. *Makes 225 g (8 oz)*

Puff Pastry

225 g (8 oz) plain flour
½ teaspoon salt
1 teaspoon lemon juice

about 1.5 dl (¼ pint) cold
  water
225 g (8 oz) butter or margarine

Sift together the flour and salt. Add the lemon juice and enough water to mix to a soft dough. Soften the butter or margarine and re-form into an oblong. Roll out the dough to a rectangle about 30 x 20 cm (12 x 8 inches) and place the butter in the centre. Fold the ends to the centre, like a parcel, to cover the butter, press the centre edges and sides to seal.

Turn the pastry a quarter of a circle and roll out to a rectangle again. Mark the dough into three and fold the lower third up and the top third down, like an envelope. Seal the edges, put the dough into a polythene bag in the fridge. Take the dough out of the bag, give it a half turn and repeat the rolling and folding 6 times allowing it to rest in the fridge for 10 minutes every second rolling. Refrigerate for 1 hour before using. *Makes 225 g (8 oz)*

White sauce

25 g (1 oz) butter or mar-
    garine
25 g (1 oz) flour

3 dl (½ pint) milk, or milk
    and fish or meat stock
salt and pepper

Melt the butter or margarine in a saucepan. Stir in the flour
and cook for about a minute over a low heat. Remove from
the heat and gradually stir in the milk, or the milk and fish or
meat stock. Return to the heat and bring to the boil, stirring
all the time. Season to taste.   *Makes 3 dl (½ pint)*

Cheese sauce: add 75 g (3 oz) grated cheese.

Béchamel sauce: add to a generous 3 dl (½ pint) milk, a bay
leaf, 3 peppercorns, 1 blade of mace, a few parsley stalks, a
piece of carrot and ½ an onion. Simmer for 10 minutes.
Strain. Make sauce as above.

French Dressing

A good French dressing can make or mar a salad and personally I think it is one of the most difficult things to make really
well, although some people just seem to have the knack of
always making a good dressing. First the ingredients are very
important; although it is more expensive I do prefer to use
olive oil and if you eat a lot of salads you may find it worth
investing in a large can of oil as this definitely saves money.
You can also use corn or vegetable oil and for some salads,
such as a pasta salad, I think this is nicer than an olive oil
dressing. Use wine vinegar, cider vinegar or lemon juice and
always use sea salt and freshly milled black pepper.

    The proportions of vinegar to oil are very largely a matter
of choice, some people like 1 tablespoon of vinegar to 2 of oil:
I prefer a slightly higher ratio of oil, about 3 or 4 to 1. Other
than the oil and seasoning you can also add a very small
quantity of French mustard, a pinch of sugar or a little honey
if you like your dressing slightly sweet, chopped fresh or dried
herbs and/or garlic. As French dressing keeps well (unless

there are a number of freshly chopped herbs added) make a large quantity in a screw-topped bottle or jar so you won't have to make it up fresh every time you want some.

Mayonnaise

Home-made mayonnaise is both cheaper and better tasting than bought. It keeps well in the fridge in a covered container, so it's worth-while making it up in quantity. Personally I prefer to make mayonnaise with corn oil, but for economy vegetable oil may be used.

2 egg yolks (or 1 whole egg if
   using a blender)*
salt and freshly milled black
   pepper

½ teaspoon French mustard
2 tablespoons wine vinegar
3 dl (½ pint) oil

Put the egg yolks, seasoning, mustard and 1 tablespoon of vinegar into a basin. Using a wooden spoon or a balloon whisk, mix until well blended. Beat in about half the oil gradually, drop by drop, until the mixture begins to look thick and shiny. Beat in the remainder of the oil a little more quickly. Then beat in the remaining vinegar. Taste and adjust seasoning. *Makes 3 dl (½ pint)*

*If you have a blender, and prefer a lighter, less rich mayonnaise, substitute 1 whole egg for the 2 egg yolks.

Pancake Batter

This quantity of pancake batter will make 8 x 17.5 cm (7 inch) pancakes. If you want to freeze cooked pancakes add a tablespoon of oil to the batter.

100 g (4 oz) flour
¼ teaspoon salt

1 egg
3 dl (½ pint) milk

Sift the flour and salt into a bowl. Add the egg, then gradually beat in half the milk to make a smooth batter. Beat in the remaining milk, then pour the batter into a jug.

Index